The POWER Series

BOMB SQUADS

S. F. Tomajczyk

MBI Publishing Company

First published in 1999 by MBI Publishing Company, PO Box 1, 729 Prospect Avenue, Osceola, WI 54020-0001 USA

MBI Publishing Company books are also available at discounts in bulk quantity for industrial or sales-promotional use. For details write to Special Sales Manager at Motorbooks International Wholesalers & Distributors, 729 Prospect Avenue, PO Box 1, Osceola, WI 54020-0001 USA.

Library of Congress Cataloging-in-Publication Data

Tomajczyk, Stephen F.
    Bomb Squads / S.F. Tomajczyk
        p. cm. -- (Power series)
    Includes index.
    ISBN 0-7603-0560-9 (paperback : alk. paper)
    1. Police--United States--Special weapons and tactics units.
2. Bombing investigation--United States.
3. Ordnance disposal units--United States. I.Title.
II. Series: Power series (Osceola, Wis.)
HV8080.S64T66 1999
363.25'964--dc21   98-50756

On the front cover: Despite the high-tech equipment and protective gear at the disposal of this bomb technician he knows that every day he shows up for work may be his last. Dedication like that is the only thing standing between us and the mayhem that terrorists and criminals create with explosive devices. *SF Tomajczyk*

On the frontispiece: Seven sticks of dynamite with a mercury switch trigger create a low-tech terrorist weapon that is easy to hide just about anywhere. It can do tremendous damage and influence national policies. *SF Tomajczyk*

On the title page: Bomb disposal is an inherently dangerous occupation. If a bomb tech isn't alert and makes a mistake, he may never know it. Bombs kill by shredding you to death with fragments and shrapnel, and by pummeling your vital organs with tremendous blast pressures that instantly turns them to mush. *Federal Bureau of Investigation*

On the back cover: This bomb tech is setting up a PAN disrupter to disarm a bomb hidden in this briefcase. He has already examined the case with an x-ray imager and knows exactly where the disrupter charge must be aimed to render the bomb safe. *SF Tomajczyk*

Edited by Christopher Batio
Designed by Dan Perry

Printed in Hong Kong

Table of Contents

A memorial to military EOD technicians killed in the line of duty is currently located at the joint military bomb school at Indian Head, Maryland. It will eventually be moved to Site 51 at Eglin Air Force Base in Florida, the new headquarters of EOD training. *NAVSCOLEOD*

For Joyce

Dedicated to the men and women who willingly walk toward danger so that others may live. You keep us safe.

And

In memory of those hazardous devices technicians who have fallen in the line of duty: 164 Military Explosive Ordnance Disposal Technicians; Brian J. Murray, New York City Police Department; Arleigh E. McCree, Los Angeles Police Department; Ronald L. Ball, Los Angeles Police Department; David B. Pulling, Delaware State Police; Jeremiah J. Hurley, Jr., Boston Police Department; and Richard Scheunning, Oregon State Police.

An Important Note From The Author

To prevent terrorists and would-be bombers from learning something that would enable them to build a deadly explosive device, I have omitted information that discusses security perimeter distances, bomb construction methods, actual render-safe procedures, effective explosive charges, bomb placement strategies, and the capability limits of counterbomb equipment. There is no need for the average reader to have this information, but a terrorist could easily make deadly use of it.

For instance, if I revealed that a department's standard safety perimeter was 50 feet, then all a bomber would have to do is build a bomb meant to destroy everything within a 100-foot radius. And if I said that most "soak times" are 5 minutes, then a bomber could construct his bomb to have a 10-minute delay. This is why I do not want to disclose sensitive information like this.

I sincerely hope that you understand the need to maintain security about some bomb disposal methods, techniques and procedures. I believe the book you are about to read will not suffer because of this, and the lives of American citizens—especially the lives of bomb technicians and first responders across the nation—depend on it.

Acknowledgments

The world of the bomb technician is a world filled with stress, suspicion, and moments of sheer terror. It is a world where intelligent and highly skilled men and women walk *toward* an explosive device to disarm it, knowing that it could kill them if they touch the wrong thing, make the wrong decision, or cut the wrong wire. It is a world where the unexpected always shows up and where the threat posed by terrorists changes as fast as technology advances. From pipe bombs to homemade nuclear devices and from mercury switches to radio frequency detonators, this book tells the story of hazardous devices technicians, brave, selfless individuals who stand between us and the evil in our society.

For me to have been allowed to become part of this deadly serious world—albeit for a very short time—was a great honor. I met a number of men and women who gained my respect and admiration for the things they do on a daily basis. I am in debt to the following people and agencies for the assistance they enthusiastically gave me in researching this book and for ensuring that I accurately portrayed their world while not giving out any secrets that would give lunatics an upper hand.

First and foremost, I'd like to extend my greatest appreciation and thanks to David L. Heaven, Supervisory Special Agent of the FBI's Hazardous Devices School (HDS). It was he who held the magical keys to the bomb technicians' kingdom and who gladly opened the door and guided me through this realm. A former Green Beret and a veteran of the Oklahoma City bombing investigation, he patiently answered my questions and introduced me to key players around the nation.

Just another day on the job. Captain Gil Udell of the U.S. Capitol Police's bomb squad, dressed in a Med-Eng Systems bomb suit and armed with a PAN disrupter, heads down range toward a suspicious package. In the background is a blue total-containment vessel. This scene is repeated hundreds of times every day by bomb technicians around the country. *SF Tomajczyk*

Others who deserve to be recognized for their contributions to this book include: Ray Funderburg, Deputy Chief, HDS; Stanley D. Setzer, Explosive Test Operator, HDS; Jose M. Colmenares, Instructor, HDS; Steve Veyera, Chief, FBI Bomb Data Center; Andy Dorman, Training Section, FBI Bomb Data Center; Ray Lopez, Operations Section, FBI Bomb Data Center; Kendrick Williams, FBI Intelligence Section; Tom Warren, FBI Bomb Data Center; Jamie Atherton, Special Agent, FBI; Neal Schiff, Public Affairs Specialist, FBI; Don P. Haldimann, Special Agent, Bomb Technician, FBI Atlanta Field Office; Bill Jonkey, Special Agent, Bomb Technician, FBI Carson City, NV, Office; Roger C. Stanton, Special Agent, FBI, Columbia, South Carolina; Art Resnick, Program Manager, Office of Public Information, ATF; Joe Dougherty, Office of Public Information, ATF; Tara Bedford, Office of Public Information, ATF; John Ryan, Office of Public Information, ATF; Special Agent Jeffrey R. Roehm, Chief, Public Information Division, ATF; Special Agent Patrick D. Hynes, Assistant Director, ATF; Special Agent Rhonda Bokorney, Chief, Canine Operations Branch, ATF; Richard A. Strobel, Forensic Chemist and Chief, Explosives Section, National Laboratory, ATF; Cynthia L. Wallace, Forensic Chemist, National Laboratory, ATF; Dondi O. Albritton, Chief, Explosives Technology Branch, ATF; Joseph C. Lund, Sr., Explosives Enforcement Officer, ETB, ATF; David S. Shatzer, Explosives Enforcement Officer, ETB, ATF; Johnnie Green, Explosives Enforcement Officer, ETB, ATF; Stephen B. Scheid, Explosives Specialist, ETB, ATF; Mark S. James, Special Agent in Charge, Intelligence Analysis Branch, ATF; Shawn C. Crawford, Canine Trainer, ATF; Robert Noll, Explosives Enforcement Officer, Canine Training Program, ATF; Carl Vasilko, Project Officer, National Response Team, ATF; District Chief Brian S. Geraci, Assistant Fire Marshal, Montgomery County, Maryland, Department of Fire & Rescue Services; Lieutenant Wayne Shaw and K-9 Tipper, Fire Investigator, Montgomery County, Maryland, Department of Fire & Rescue Services; Captain Sam Hsu, Fire Investigator, Montgomery County, Maryland, Department of Fire & Rescue Services; POIII John M. Binnix, Canine Section, Montgomery County, Maryland, Police Department; Lisa Gordon-Haggerty, Director, Office of Emergency Response, Department of Energy; Roxanne Dey, PAO, Nuclear Emergency Search Team, Department of Energy; Captain Fiske, SSG "B.J." Bjorkman, SSG Guerrero, and SSG McCarthy of the U.S. Army Ordnance Missile & Munitions Center & School, Redstone Arsenal; Colonel Mary G. Goodwin, CO, 52nd Ordnance Group; Master Sergeant John Simpson, 52nd Ordnance Group; Major James J. Shivers, Operations Officer, 52nd Ordnance Group; Lieutenant Colonel Mike Perez, CO, 184th Ordnance Battalion, U.S. Army; Captain Pirkle, Sergeant Todd Hunter, Sergeant Carpenter and Sergeant Peters of the 723rd Ordnance Company, U.S. Army; SSG Jacob Clement, U.S. Army, ACO, Technical Escort Unit; Lieutenant Amy Derrick, PAO, Department of the U.S. Navy; Lieutenant Merritt Allen, PAO, Department of the U.S. Navy; T.J. LaPuzza, PAO, Naval Command, Control & Ocean Surveillance Center; Lieutenant Commander R.N. Wiegert, U.S. Navy, Executive Officer, NAVSCOLEOD; HT1 (EOD) Ken C. Anderson, U.S. Navy, PAO, NAVSCOLEOD; Command Master Chief Ancelet, U.S. Navy, NAVSCOLEOD; ENCS (SW/DV) Craig Settler, U.S. Navy, NAVSCOLEOD; Master Sergeant Bonnie Richardson, USAR, NAVSCOLEOD; Staff Sergeant Edward L. Patton, USAF, NAVSCOLEOD; GMC Brian Hodge, U.S. Navy, NAVSCOLEOD; OSC Mike Aramanda, U.S. Navy, Branch Head, Area 8, NAVSCOLEOD;

GMM Will Journigan, U.S. Navy, NAVS-COLEOD; GMC Craig Smith, U.S. Navy, NAVS-COLEOD; EN1 (EOD) Iron Moccasian, U.S. Navy, NAVSCOLEOD; MN1 P. Taslor, U.S. Navy, NAVSCOLEOD; GMG1 (EOD) Terrance Thomas, U.S. Navy, NAVSCOLEOD; Lisa Brown, Unabomb Task Force, U.S. Department of Justice; Mavis Dezulozich, PAO, U.S. Marshals Service; Sergeant John McMasters, Commander, New Hampshire State Police Explosive Disposal Unit (Ret.); Donald P. Bliss, State Fire Marshal and J. William Degnan, Deputy State Fire Marshal, New Hampshire Department of Safety; Mike McGroarty, Chief, City of La Habra Fire Department; Gary L. Abrecht, Chief of Police, U.S. Capitol Police; Sergeant Daniel R. Nichols, Public Information Officer, U.S. Capitol Police; Capt. Gilman G. Udell, Jr., Commander, Technical Security Division, U.S. Capitol Police; Detective Dave Novak, U.S. Capitol Police; Sergeant Ray Eaton, U.S. Capitol Police; Special Agent John King, U.S. Capitol Police; Lieutenant Mike Conway, U.S. Capitol Police; Lieutenant Shelton, U.S. Capitol Police Canine Unit; Sergeant T. J. Williams, U.S. Capitol Police Canine Unit; Norman E. Smith, President, Protection Development International Corp.; Mary Ann Smith, Executive President, Protection Development International Corp.; Glenn Hurd, President, Hurd's Custom Machinery; Randy Markey, Vice President, Nabco, Inc.; R. J. Brill, President, Royal Arms International; Richard L'Abbé, P.Eng., President, Med-Eng Systems Inc., Vince Crupi, P.Eng., Vice President of Sales and Marketing, Med-Eng Systems Inc.; Dr. Aris Makris, Ph.D., Vice President, Research and Development, Med-Eng Systems Inc.; Rosa Elena van der Stoel, Executive Assistant, Med-Eng Systems Inc.; John Carson, Marketing Coordinator, Med-Eng Systems Inc.; Steve Wampler, PIO, Lawrence Livermore National Laboratory; Larry Perrine, PIO, and John German, PIO, Sandia National Laboratory; Jo Ann Moore, Program Manager, U.S. Department of State; Fred Testa, Director, Manchester Airport; Sergeant Forbes, Rockingham County Sheriff; Sergeant Gary Hicks, University of Michigan Police; Amanda Gaylor, Rand Corporation; Mary Lamberton, Researcher, National Geographic Society; Herb Martin, President, Custom Slide Service; and Linda Walters, Intra-World Travel, Atlanta, Georgia.

My appreciation is also extended to those individuals who, because of the sensitive nature of their jobs, requested anonymity in exchange for talking with me. You know who you are, and I haven't forgotten your important contributions to this book. (Especially you, "Johnnie Walker Black Fossil Man!")

Thank you all for trusting me, and for sharing your "Never, *ever* cut the red wire" world with me. Through your efforts and the collective efforts of everyone I met and spoke with over the course of 2 years, Americans will now have a better understanding of what it is you do, and why you walk toward a bomb when everyone else is running away.

–S. F. Tomajczyk

Who in their right mind walks toward a live bomb? Bombs, after all, are not only unpredictable, they are inherently dangerous. They kill without mercy. They maim without remorse. They are the tools of mayhem and carnage.

Yet, in spite of this, some 1,000 civilian bomb technicians in America are willing to take that walk. Using high-tech tools and relying on their knowledge and experience, they take a calculated risk to snuff out a bomb before it explodes and spills the blood of innocent bystanders. Each and every day, 7 days a week, from Florida to California, in small, sleepy country towns and huge, bustling metropolitan areas, these highly trained men and women examine thousands of suspicious packages, disarm hundreds of homemade pipe bombs, and respond to dozens of actual explosions.

Unless you have been the victim of a bomber (or just happened to be near ground zero of an explosion), chances are you are unaware of just how often bombs are found. In any given year, about 2,000 bombings in the United States, an average of five each day, result in the deaths of 500 to 700 people. This distressing figure doesn't include bombing attempts, stolen explosive incidents, or hoax devices. Most of these incidents involve revenge or jealousy as the motive—a spurned lover eliminating the competition for another's

"We don't forgive. We don't forget."

–P. J. Crowley, Spokesman, National Security Council Responding to the bombing of two U.S. Embassies in Africa, August 1998

affection, an employee getting even with a supervisor, or an angry citizen wanting retribution against the government.

Because of the absolute horror a bomb creates, most of us prefer not to think about explosive devices and the types of people who would build and use them. This tactic works until an incident so monstrous occurs that we can no longer ignore the reality of our world.

Beirut.

The World Trade Center.

Oklahoma City.

Centennial Park.

Kenya.

These bombings captured the entire world's attention, not just our own. In these instances, the bomber won, using carnage and body counts to send his message. This lesson is being passed on to a new generation of terrorists.

First, bombs are becoming more sophisticated, making it more difficult for bomb technicians to disarm them. Criminals are also making their bombs more deadly by adding shrapnel (such as nails, chains, and ball bearings) to their devices, knowing full well that it will rip to shreds anyone near the bomb when it explodes.

Second, as illustrated by the 1995 Sarin gas attack in Tokyo, terrorists are now delving into the arena of chemical and biological warfare.

The World Trade Center as seen the night after the February 1993 bombing. Ramsi Yousef, who masterminded the bombing, hoped that one tower would topple like a domino into the adjacent tower, sending 100,000 people to their deaths. *Bureau of Alcohol, Tobacco & Firearms*

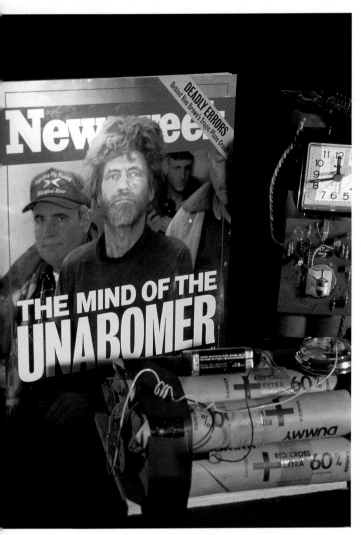

When the Unabomber, Theodore Kaczynski, was finally captured in his remote Montana cabin in April 1996, it made the front cover of magazines and newspapers around the world. Using crude bombs left in public places and sophisticated devices sent through the mail, reclusive Kaczynski confounded the FBI for 18 years. His 16 bombings, which were mostly targeted at universities and airlines across the country, killed 3 people and injured 23. Kaczynski pled guilty to the crimes and is now serving a life sentence. *SF Tomajczyk*

They are building special devices that release deadly germs and gas, which passersby can't see or smell.

And last, terrorists are going after police, firemen, EMTs and bomb techs who respond to a bombing incident. Some now hide a second bomb near the first. When first responders arrive in answer to the first bomb to help the injured and dying, the second bomb explodes, killing them.

This is the gut-wrenching reality that we are all faced with, and it is the world in which bomb technicians must do their job.

"Real-Life" Bomb Disposal

The real world of bomb disposal is not like what is portrayed on Hollywood's silver screen. Bomb techs, for instance, don't walk up to a ticking time bomb at the last minute and try to figure out which wire to cut by hand. Similarly, they don't pick up and toss a bomb into a nearby swimming pool or river. Neither do they leap away from a bomb's explosive blast (just as it's detonating, mind you) and skillfully dodge the fragments, which are traveling at speeds of 5,000 feet per second and faster.

If nothing else, movies like *Speed* and *Blown Away*, although entertaining in their own right, do a disservice to bomb technicians by not accurately depicting their truly dramatic world. Granted, we shouldn't know all the tricks and trade secrets of how they render safe a bomb, but then again neither should we be ignorant of the basic conditions under which they perform their dangerous and important jobs.

In reality, bomb disposal today is *not* a hands-on vocation. That's because a bomb can be built and triggered in many ways. Most bombs are homemade (a.k.a. improvised), and are limited in their design only by

continued on page 18

"It was apocalyptic. It was probably the most chaotic and hellacious thing I've ever seen or heard in my life."

That's how FBI agent and bomb technician Don Haldimann described the scene that greeted him when he arrived at the 110-story World Trade Center in New York on February 26, 1993. He and other FBI agents had been returning to work after an early lunch at Niños in Brooklyn when they heard sirens wailing everywhere. Using the car radio, Haldimann learned that an explosion had occurred in downtown Manhattan, so he sped to the scene.

After meeting up with Lieutenant Walter Boser of the New York City bomb squad, they went into the building's underground garage to evaluate what had caused the fire and damage that rocked the twin towers. Initially, there was speculation that a generator or gas main had exploded. The journey inside was like walking

The World Trade Center bomb was carefully placed in the underground parking garage to inflict maximum damage to the building's infrastructure. The explosion formed a crater measuring 200 feet by 100 feet, and was seven stories deep. The people and cars in this photo clearly show the scale of the bomb blast. An ATF agent is in the foreground, searching for evidence. *Bureau of Alcohol, Tobacco & Firearms*

through a nightmare. All the power was knocked out, and their only source of light came from the flashlights they held and the glow of 80 burning cars. Acrid smoke burned their eyes and choked their throats as car alarms screeched all around them. Overhead, bursting pipes showered them with water and sewage, creating fetid, knee-deep pools that they had to wade through. And, making matters worse, live electrical wires were strewn like enormous piles of spaghetti.

"It was unbelievable," says Haldimann, who cut his head on some debris. "It was really hard to talk or to see each other. Plus, it wasn't a simple matter of just walking in. We had conduits down, everything was collapsed and broken, with cars thrown up against concrete supports and wrapped around poles. We had to worm our way through all that."

When they finally reached the seat of the blast, Haldimann and Boser found a huge crater measuring 200 feet by 100 feet and falling seven stories deep. They saw burn marks on the walls and the explosive-shattered steel remnants of a large cross beam that was missing.

"We made the determination right there in the hole, around 1:30, that we had a large explosive device, probably a vehicle device, because there was no way somebody could carry in something that big and set it off."

This realization sent a shiver up Haldimann's spine. "We'd never seen anything like that in America before," he explains. Large-scale terrorism had finally arrived on our shores, and the world of the bomb technician was about to change forever.

An experienced agent, Haldimann has spent his career tracking down terrorists. He knew that they had to start working the case immediately, before the suspects got too much of a head start on them. He called FBI headquarters and had forensic examiners sent in. He also went to the Bureau of Alcohol, Tobacco and Firearms and asked for their assistance.

The bomb killed 6 and injured 1,042 people. Three of the lucky survivors were Secret Service agents who were just getting out of their cars as the bomb exploded almost next to them. They were literally blown out of their shoes and tossed up under nearby vehicles. The agents—bleeding, dazed and suffering eye and ear injuries—managed to climb out of the blast area. They commandeered a taxi at gunpoint and went to the nearest hospital for medical treatment. *Bureau of Alcohol, Tobacco & Firearms*

With himself, two ATF National Response Teams, the New York City bomb squad, and several other FBI bomb techs, they stabilized the crime scene and began searching for residues and bomb fragments. They staged their operations out of an Evidence Control Center that was set up in the basement of the Merrill Lynch building, half a block from the World Trade Center.

Evidence was collected at the crater, bagged and then transported in vans to a secure location in the city. Some of the evidence was examined at the New York City police department's lab; the rest was sent to the FBI's laboratory in Washington, D.C. All remaining debris was scooped up by a bulldozer, loaded on a flatcar and transported to a warehouse in New Jersey.

Since this was the first major bombing in America, there was some uncertainty as to what might be important evidence, and what was just debris. "We didn't know what to collect and what not to collect," says Haldimann. "We didn't know how the prosecution was going to go. So we erred on the side of caution and seized everything. We ended up with 10 to 20 tons of stuff we really didn't need. We got explosively damaged wood, concrete, you name it. We didn't need all that stuff. All we really need is the explosively damaged vehicle, the container and the parts of the IED (improvised explosive device)."

Search teams were looking for evidence in many different areas of the crater. "We had as many as seven teams, anywhere from 5 to 12 guys each, working." They worked 20 hours per day in shifts, with 4 hours off to sleep.

Two days after the explosion, they knew a vehicle bomb was responsible for the blast. Specifically, a bomb was placed inside a Ford Econoline E-350 Ryder van that had been parked 1 to 2 feet away from the wall of the World Trade Center in the garage. The key piece of evidence was a twisted, 72-inch part of the vehicle's framework that had a Confidential Vehicle Identification Number stamped on it. The piece was found by ATF bomb tech Joseph Hanlin and NYPD detective Don Sadowy, who were searching an area near the seat of the explosion.

Using the CVIN, the FBI was able to track the van through Ryder to the place it had been rented and the person who signed it out. They subsequently arrested Mohammed Salameh, 25, when he returned to Ryder to get his $400 deposit back. He was just the first of many men who would be arrested in this bombing plot.

Meanwhile, the Crime Scene Team had a van identical to the one used in the bombing brought into the crater. They also arranged for a Ford engineer and an auto crime specialist from the New York City Auto Crime Unit to dismantle portions of the van and compare its pieces with those from the blast scene. This prevented the bomb techs from confusing van parts with pieces of a shattered Toyota or Cadillac.

Now that they knew where the explosion had occurred, the investigators had to determine the type and amount of explosive material used, and how the bomb was constructed. Residue tests from the crater eventually confirmed the bomb was made with urea nitrate. This was further proven when the FBI raided a house in New Jersey where the terrorists had made the explosive by cooking down a mixture of urea, sulfuric acid and nitric acid. This process, which is very caustic, left all the metal in the house rusted, including the

The terrorists packed 1,200 pounds of urea nitrate into a Ryder van like this one, and triggered it with homemade nitroglycerin. After an ATF agent and a NYPD detective found a piece of the vehicle containing a Confidential Vehicle Identification Number, the FBI was able to track the van to the person who rented it and arrest him. *Federal Bureau of Investigation*

sheetrock nails (which were under a coat of paint). When the FBI set out to duplicate the explosive mixture at Eglin Air Force Base in Florida, the resulting fumes caused agents to bleed from the nose and mouth.

Investigative efforts revealed that the terrorists had bought 1,500 pounds of urea. By the time they cooked it down into the explosive—urea nitrate—there was about 1,300 pounds left. The terrorists used homemade nitroglycerin to set it off. The FBI was able to prove this shortly after Salameh's arrest, when they received a call from the manager of a self-storage facility in Jersey City, New Jersey. He had seen Salameh's photo in the newspapers and told agents that the suspect was renting one of his storage units.

Although it was nearing midnight and snowing outside, Don Haldimann, officers from the New Jersey State Police and the Jersey City Police Department Bomb Squad immediately went to the storage unit to search it. Two ATF forensic chemists accompanied them to identify anything in the room that could be used as an explosive component. When the storage door was opened, they discovered several barrels of sulfuric acid, nitric acid and containers with unknown liquids of various colors. There was also some unused urea. All of the items were carefully packed into 11 containers and then transported by bomb trailers to Jersey State Park, a cook-off point.

At the same time, an FBI chemist took a sample of one of the unknown liquids and ran it back to the lab in New York City for analysis. Several hours later, Don Haldimann's cell phone rang. It was 2 A.M. and he was standing next to the bomb trailers with snow swirling around him. "NG! NG!" screamed the lab tech into the phone.

Don paused. "NG? No good?"

"No! NG!" the tech shouted, "Nitroglycerin!"

Haldimann's stomach tightened. "What happens when it's exposed to cold temps?" he asked. It was 15 degrees outside, and falling.

"Don't get anywhere close to it," the lab tech warned. "It crystallizes. The crystals get real long. You never know when it will sympathetically detonate. Don't get any of your guys near it."

That was enough for Haldimann. He had police immediately evacuate the area. Then he and the bomb techs regrouped to discuss how to handle the situation. They knew that the terrorists' fingerprints were likely on the nitroglycerin containers, but they also knew that nitro is extremely sensitive and even more temperamental in freezing temperatures. To try to "lift" fingerprints off the containers would be a suicide mission. In the end, they decided to use C-4 plastic explosive to countercharge several pounds of nitroglycerin. After moving back about a mile, they let it go. The explosion destroyed the New Jersey State Police's open-vent bomb trailer.

Haldimann remained on the case until March 28, when the crime scene was officially turned over to the Port Authority. Through the collective postblast efforts of the FBI, ATF and local police, they had uncovered the evidence necessary to eventually convict the terrorists who had killed six people, injured more than 1,000 and caused $550 million in damage.

Officials later revealed that the World Trade Center was just the opening shot of a planned Islamic Holy War against the United States. Other Muslim extremists had plotted to blow up the United Nations, the New York offices of the FBI, and the Holland and Lincoln tunnels in July 1993. They also plotted to assassinate four politicians, including the UN Secretary General and U.S. Senator Alfonse D'Amato of New York.

Although the horrific plans were thwarted by the FBI, they were nothing compared to what Ramsi Yousef, the mastermind of the World Trade Center bombing, was planning. Yousef fled the United States on the night of the bombing, leaving behind letters condemning American support of Israel and threatening more violence. While

To help remove the tons of debris from the crater, a bulldozer (shown here) was disassembled, dropped through a hole cut in the sidewalk between the Vista Hotel and the World Trade Center, and then reassembled. Evidence was taken to a nearby command post for analysis. *Federal Bureau of Investigation*

evading a worldwide manhunt by flying between countries using several aliases, he created a plan, codenamed "Bojinka," to blow up 12 U.S. passenger planes in a 48-hour period over the Pacific Ocean. He hoped his plan would kill 4,000 people.

On December 11, 1994, a coconspirator, Abdul Murad, placed a small bomb on a Philippines Airline flight bound for Tokyo. It exploded while the plane was flying over Okinawa, killing a 24-year-old Japanese passenger and injuring 10 others. Amazingly, the plane was not destroyed, and it landed safely. The event was a trial run for the real plan the following month. However, fortune worked against the bombers. While mixing explosives at Murad's apartment in Manila, Yousef started a fire that brought police and firemen to the scene. He fled, leaving Murad behind along with incriminating evidence, including a computer that contained the flight schedules for Delta, Northwest and United flights bound for the United States from the Far East.

Yousef was arrested in Islamabad, Pakistan, in February 1995 and was returned to the United States. On the trip back, he gave FBI agents a 56-page account of the World Trade Center bombing, including details on how the bomb was made.

In January 1998, Ramsi Yousef was sentenced to life in solitary confinement, plus 240 years for his terrorist activities. In handing down the sentence, U.S. District Judge Kevin Duffy called Yousef an "apostle of evil," a title that may, sadly, be passed on to future terrorist bombers.

continued from page 12

the imagination of the bomber and the resources available to him. Over the years, bombers have used a variety of components to build bombs, including mercury switches, bare bulb initiators, Pyrodex, radio frequency triggers, pressure switches, blasting caps, nitroglycerin dynamite, passive infrared sensors, and photoelectric cells.

In fact, the possibility of finding a bomb that looks like a stereotypical movie bomb is nearly nonexistent. Even the basic pipe bomb has hundreds of ways to rig it, with no version considered standard. This is reinforced by one 96-page book on the market today that shows dozens of pipe bomb schematics.

The only common denominator that exists among bombs is that they are designed to explode.

Because of this, no bomb tech wants to touch a device, much less pick it up and cradle it. Bomb disposal, which in decades past was a macho "hands-on, cut any wire" profession, has metamorphosed into a remote, high-tech "safety first" occupation. Anyone without this cautious attitude will not survive very long.

Whenever possible, the modern bomb tech relies on robots and other stand-off tools to examine and disarm a bomb. He never forgets that when it comes to explosives, distance is his best friend. The only time he comes close to the explosive device in person is to take an X-ray of it and to set up the disrupter, a gun-like tool that prevents the bomb from functioning as designed. And even in these instances, he wears an armored bomb suit like the Med-Eng EOD-7B, and he makes sure to get away from the bomb as quickly as possible.

With advancements in technology, today's bomb technicians have to be experts in electronics, hazardous materials, wiring systems, explosives, power sources, chemical and biological warfare agents, nuclear power, and

To get the public's attention, terrorist-bombers are adding shrapnel to their bombs, knowing that it will result in bloodier incidents and higher body counts. As this photo reveals, shrapnel can be anything from marbles to nails. In fact, the bomb that exploded at Centennial Olympic Park in 1996 had 6 pounds of masonry nails added to it by the bomber. *SF Tomajczyk*

triggering technologies (e.g., microwave, acoustic, seismic). They also have to be proficient in using and operating their equipment, such as the bomb suit, an X-ray source, the bomb trailer and rigging tools. Furthermore, they must understand the numerous render-safe procedures that exist, which provide a step-by-step process to safely disarm a particular explosive device.

Indeed, the so-called "Bomb Disposal Two Step" has become a dance of increasing complexity. In this profession, you can never have a bad day. If you do, you might not go home.

Special People, Special Crises

It goes without saying that it takes a special breed of person to want to get involved in bomb disposal. Generally speaking, bomb techs are intelligent and insightful individuals who are patient, flexible team players. They enjoy working with their hands—tinkering with gadgets out of curiosity—and they possess the ability to see things in three dimensions, a useful trait when figuring out how a bomb is constructed. They also get a rush out of living life on the edge, working under pressure, and playing a mental chess game with the bomber. In the end, only they and the bomber really know how a particular device was built and how it can be disarmed.

Some 1,000 civilian bomb techs and 3,000 military EOD technicians live and work in the United States. Together, they are responsible for keeping 260 million Americans safe from the terrorists and bombers inside America and around the world. The training these individuals undergo to become certified bomb techs is extremely rigorous; in the following pages, we will explore the ways they are taught to examine and disarm a wide variety of explosive devices. You will meet several bomb squads up close and personal and be introduced to several

The bombing of the Murrah Federal Building in Oklahoma City killed 168 people, including several children who were staying at America's Kids, a government-operated day care center located on the second floor. The grief Americans felt caused them to spontaneously place wreaths and toys at the site of the bombing. Timothy McVeigh was convicted of the bombing and is serving a life sentence. *Mike McGroarty*

Lightly defended targets: That's what terrorists look for to ensure their attack is successful. The June 1996 bombing of U.S. military personnel living in Khobar Towers on King Abdul Aziz Air Base in Saudi Arabia exemplifies this. The building was located right next to a main road. The terrorists simply drove up in a fuel truck and ran off before it exploded with the force of 20,000 pounds of TNT. This picture shows piles of evidence recovered from the blast. The huge bomb crater is located behind the piles. *U.S. Department of Defense*

of the little-known, yet most dangerous, bombing incidents that these units have responded to over the years. You will also see and read about the plethora of high-tech tools that technicians rely on to render safe bombs while staying alive in the process.

The book ends with a unique look at the threat posed by "super terrorism"—an attack involving improvised nuclear devices or chemical and biological agents. You'll learn that the United States has tried to respond to such a threat by forming the Nuclear Emergency Search Team, the Technical Escort Unit, the Chemical/Biological Incident Response Force and the Army's special Weapons of Mass Destruction (WMD) Response Teams, which are part of the 52nd Ordnance Group. However, even with all these elite units, the initial response to a bomb threat or explosion will always weigh on the shoulders of the local bomb squad and first responders. It is to them that we owe our lives and our thanks. And it is to them that this book is ultimately dedicated.

The idea was born at the 1995 Super Bowl in Atlanta. At the 2-minute warning in the fourth quarter, two bomb threats came into the stadium at the same time. Both callers identified an area at the 50-yard line in the underground electrical bus tunnel as having a bomb. Because of the seeming legitimacy, on-scene bomb techs from the FBI, Georgia Bureau of Investigation and the Atlanta Police Department scrambled to respond. Before they reached the field to begin evacuating the football players, however, they were met by two other bomb techs who had been watching the game from the sidelines. When they had heard the call-out on their radios, they quickly checked the nearby tunnel and cleared it. There was no bomb.

This incident—and the manner in which it was so quickly handled—gave FBI Special Agent Don Haldimann a great idea. Tasked with overseeing bomb disposal efforts at the 1996 Atlanta Olympics, Haldimann realized that what he had just witnessed could be put to effective use at the Games. His idea was to place four-man "counterbomb" teams at every Olympic venue in order to quickly evaluate and diagnose suspicious items. They would wear civilian clothes so as not to alarm the public. If the item turned out to be a bomb, they would immediately evacuate the area, set up a perimeter and guide a bomb disposal team directly to the device. This would eliminate wasted time and save lives.

It seemed like a fine idea. Counterbomb efforts would be proactive instead of reactive. Hence, the Explosive Diagnostic Team (EDT) concept was born. Each EDT comprised four people: two EOD techs from the Army's 52nd Ordnance Group, a FBI Bomb Technician and an ATF Certified Explosives Specialist. The 24 teams provided coverage at all 43 Olympic-sanctioned venues.

Complementing their efforts were 24 teams of bomb-sniffing dogs and a slew of response teams trained in dealing with weapons of mass destruction. Additionally, Navy EOD divers were responsible for checking the Olympic venues for sailing and kayaking, and U.S. Postal Inspection Service agents who screened all Olympic mail. All of this effort was supported by an aviation unit of UH-1 Huey and UH-60 Black Hawk helicopters that could quickly fly bomb techs to and from any Olympic venue.

The bombing of Centennial Olympic Park in 1996 left one woman dead and more than 100 injured, and it marred the peace of the Olympic Games. The bomb, consisting of three pipe bombs and 6 pounds of nails, was hidden inside an Army-style backpack and left at the base of the ATT/NBC Tower, shown here. The bomb crater is located under the furthest tent awning to the left. *52nd Ordnance Group*

A closer look at the "blast seat" where the bomb exploded. The bomb was discovered just before it detonated, but not early enough to evacuate the crowd of people that had gathered there to listen to a rock band. *52nd Ordnance Group*

If a bomb exploded, the ATF's National Response Team and FBI's Evidence Response Teams were on hand to conduct the postblast investigation. All of these units were controlled and deployed by the Bomb Management Center (BMC) at Dobbins Air Reserve Base in Marietta, just northwest of Atlanta. The system was organized very effectively: The Explosive Diagnostic Teams were tasked with taking a "first look" at a suspicious package and determining if a threat existed. If it did, they would notify the BMC, which would decide what action should be taken.

If time was of the essence, the item could be immediately disarmed by the EDT members, who had basic bomb disposal tools (i.e., bomb suit, disrupter, X-ray set, tool kit). Otherwise, the BMC would dispatch a better-equipped Render Safe Procedure team (RSP team) to the site. The four six-man RSP teams were based at the BMC and were equipped with robots, bomb trailers, disrupters, X-ray systems, fluoroscope machines, fiber optic systems, electronic stethoscopes, and demolition kits.

During the 36 days of the Olympic Games, more than 2,000 suspicious items were examined by the Explosive Diagnostic Teams. In 15 cases, the item was considered dangerous enough to require using a disrupter.

"We shot suspect packages if they had any components that we didn't recognize exactly as what they were, especially if we had wires and we had other stuff in there that led us to believe that we had an explosive device," says Haldimann.

In one instance, a box was found to contain railroad flares, which on an X-ray resemble sticks of dynamite. Another time, a box that was dealt with turned out to be CO_2 canisters filled with black powder. And still another potential bomb was disrupted and later found to be a dummy bomb used by the United Parcel Service to test their X-ray operators.

But with all the false alarms the RSP teams dealt with in Atlanta, one device was very real. What everyone will remember from the 1996 Olympics is the bomb that exploded at Centennial Olympic Park, killing one woman and injuring dozens of bystanders. The explosion occurred around 1:20 A.M. on July 27. Although the park was not an Olympic-sanctioned venue, police were on hand to monitor the crowd that was listening to a rock band. Georgia Bureau of Investigation agent Tom Davis spotted a green army-like backpack lying at the base of the AT&T/NBC Tower, and called for an Explosive Diagnostic Team to investigate. ATF agent Steve "Fuzzy" Zellers and FBI agent Bill Forsythe responded to the call. Opening up the backpack, they saw three pipe bombs and a lot of wire. They notified the Bomb Management Center that they had found a confirmed IED, and immediately began evacuating people out of the park with the assistance of other police officers. While they did that, the center deployed RSP Team Number Two . . . but it was too late.

Zellers and Forsythe were about 25 or 30 feet from the bomb when it exploded. However, because they were downhill from the backpack at the time, and because the bomber had affixed a metal plate to the bomb (this caused the blast to be directed slightly upward) neither of them was injured. The bomb fragments, including 6 pounds of masonry nails, flew over their heads. However, Alice S. Hawthorne, a 44-year-old mother of two daughters from Albany, Georgia, wasn't as fortunate. Standing 80 feet from the bomb, she suffered extensive shrapnel wounds and died on the spot. More than 100 other bystanders were injured.

"There were a lot of nails," says ATF forensic chemist Richard Strobel. "It's pretty amazing that it wasn't worse than what it was. They definitely were trying to kill an awful lot of people with that device."

Don Haldimann, who had just gone to bed, was awakened by a phone call from the BMC. Within 45 minutes, he was on the scene. He told the police and firemen to leave the dead woman in place and get the injured out of the immediate area. Dog teams and bomb techs were brought in to sweep the park for secondary devices and unconsumed explosives. At the same time, FBI special agents from the Atlanta Joint Terrorism Task Force were sent to the hospitals to collect evidence from the wounded, such as bomb fragments lodged in their skin, and residue on clothing and personal belongings.

By 4:30 A.M. the park was declared free of explosives. Hawthorne's body was removed by the medical examiner's office after being photographed and documented in place. By 6:30 A.M. the postblast investigation was well under way.

Although the investigation has had its twists and turns since then, FBI and ATF officials today believe there is a strong similarity among bombs used at Centennial Olympic Park and devices targeted at an Alabama abortion clinic and a Georgia night club. The prime suspect in the case is Army veteran Eric Robert Rudolph, who has been charged in the fatal January 1998 abortion clinic blast. He fled into the remote mountains of western North Carolina after that incident, and has evaded capture in the months since. As of January 1999, he is on the FBI's 10 Most Wanted List, and a $1 million reward is offered for his arrest.

There it was—a weathered and innocent-looking 36-foot-long trailer sitting in a forest opening. Yet the bomb technician who was approaching it knew better. Intelligence reports had the trailer pegged as a drug laboratory, and that meant danger. Before taking each step, the bomb tech scanned the ground ahead of him for trip wires and pressure plates. Clan labs (as clandestine drug labs are known) are notorious for containing booby traps. In many cases, it is a death-defying accomplishment for a bomb tech to safely reach the lab's front door. Being able to check inside the structure for explosive chemicals and improvised devices is considered a bonus.

Many bomb techs hate clan lab assignments for this very reason. Potential death is everywhere you look, so you can't afford to have your concentration wane for even a split second. This particular bomb tech knew that. He carefully stepped over a length of trip wire hidden in the tall grass—booby trap No. 9—and then checked under the trailer's metal steps before climbing to the front door. He instinctively reached for the door handle and then froze.

"Idiot," he scolded himself and then slipped a length of thin rope over the handle, backed away to the side several feet and gave

> **"There is an inherent danger in EOD work . . . so you kind of want to know what you're doing."**
>
> –Raymond O. Funderburg, Deputy Chief, HDS

the rope a gentle pull. The handle turned and the door slowly swung opened. Nothing happened. He waited a few minutes, just to be safe. Delayed triggers aren't uncommon.

When nothing happened, he took a deep breath and entered the trailer. What he saw through the thick visor of his bomb suit made him whistle in surprise. The living room and kitchen were cluttered with beakers, test tubes and canisters filled with unknown chemicals. Yellow liquids, blue powders, green gels, and sticks of orange dynamite. The room was like a scene from a mad scientist's lab. The bomb tech stood in awe, overwhelmed by the task ahead of him. It would take hours to check each container and remove it from the building.

He took a half step toward the kitchen . . . and in the split second before the booby trap exploded, he knew that he had stepped on a pressure plate hidden beneath the thin carpeting.

Click.

BOOOOOOOOOOOOM!

$%#@!!

He was dead.

"Don't feel bad," an instructor nearby told him, grinning from ear to ear. "Nearly everyone dies in this exercise. We stacked the deck against you."

For the next several minutes, the instructor lectures the embarrassed bomb tech about

A student is ready to try his hand at X-raying a suspicious device. In his right hand is a portable Golden X-ray system; in his left, a film pack. His goal is to vertically place the film pack as close as possible behind the bomb, without actually touching it. The X-ray source is placed on the opposite side, and a "picture" is taken. A few minutes later, the innards of the bomb are revealed, and the bomb tech can figure out how to disarm it. *SF Tomajczyk*

Punching holes in an explosive is not recommended, unless you know what you're doing . . . as this student obviously does. He's threaded Geldyne with det-cord, which can be used to blow up many things. *SF Tomajczyk*

what he did wrong and what entry procedure he should have followed. This way, he won't make the same mistake ever again. And, because of it, he'll live longer when he returns to the real world in a few weeks.

Welcome to the FBI's Hazardous Devices School (HDS), where every civilian bomb technician in America receives his formal training. Located at the Army's Redstone Arsenal in Huntsville, Alabama, the Hazardous Devices School teaches its students about explosive charges and devices and how to render them safe without getting killed in the process. The five-week basic training course is arduous, but given the topic that's being taught, hard work is to be expected. After all, if you fail here, chances are good that you'll die "out there." Hence, the instructors at HDS expect every single student to take bomb disposal and render-safe procedures very seriously.

The Selection Process

Established in January 1971, HDS teaches bomb techs everything from explosives recognition, bomb safety and nomenclature to advanced topics like dealing with chemical and biological weapons.

"We basically start off with the thought that the individual knows nothing," says Ray Funderburg, a retired Army master sergeant who helps oversee the operations of the school as its deputy chief. He says that even though most HDS students "are very sharp," the course really starts with the basics.

It's an important point, since the students attending the school have varied backgrounds. Some, for instance, have gone through local training seminars or have been working on their local bomb squad as an assistant for a year or longer. They have an idea of what bomb disposal is all about, while other students are complete novices when it comes to explosives.

To attend HDS, a student has to be recommended by his local bomb squad commander and be approved by his department's chief executive. He also has to have five years

BLAM! There's nothing that a few pounds of high explosives can't cure. Get too close though, and you become a pink cloud. Students get a lot of hands-on training at HDS' field ranges in how to safely use explosives to countercharge hazardous devices. Eye and ear protection is required for all students, instructors and guests. *SF Tomajczyk*

of law enforcement experience under his belt, with at least another five years of service ahead of him. Due to the rigorous nature of the training conducted at HDS, a candidate *must* be in excellent physical condition. Students are not accepted for training if they have health problems, such as a hearing loss greater than 60 decibels, abnormal EKG readings, a seizure disorder, high blood pressure, or if they are overweight.

Instructors take the last two conditions very seriously because there is a distinct correlation between a person being overweight with high blood pressure and his likelihood of having a heart attack when responding to a bomb call. An individual with these problems is also more prone to heat stress as a result of wearing a heavy bomb suit. The last thing you want to do is to send in EMTs to rescue a bomb tech who has collapsed next to a bomb.

The selection of candidates for attendance at HDS is based on the availability of space in a particular class. Generally, there are only 24 students per class to ensure quality, one-on-one training. Small classes mean the instructors can keep a close eye on what the students are doing and can quickly correct them before a mistake is made. This is especially important when they are working with live explosives.

HDS also considers the pressing needs of the candidate's department, the number of existing bomb techs in the candidate's area, and whether or not the candidate will have access to the proper bomb-disposal tools when he returns home. This equipment issue is important. HDS doesn't want to train someone who won't be able to do the job properly because of a lack of equipment.

Because of this competitive selection process, some candidates to have to wait 12 to 18 months after applying before attending the school. As of 1998, more than 6,000 bomb technicians had been trained at HDS.

The so-called "Dead Bug Drill" has HDS students lying flat on their backs and struggling to their feet while wearing a 60-pound bomb suit. As this photo shows, it takes flexibility and Frankenstein-like motions to accomplish this. Students quickly learn that a bomb suit is not as bulky and cumbersome as they first thought. *SF Tomajczyk*

Welcome to Hard Work

The Basic Course is broken down into three phases. The first phase gives students training in conventional explosives (e.g., dynamite, C-4) and improvised explosives (e.g., urea nitrate). Conventional explosives are usually manufactured for commercial or military use, while improvised explosives are made (often for criminal purposes) from items such as fertilizer and fuel oil, which were never intended to be used in a bomb. The students work with these materials daily so they become intimately familiar with them. Why? Because they'll be using them in all aspects of

No, it's not prayer time. These students are practicing how to do delicate and precise actions while wearing a bomb suit. After putting on their suits, they walk 300 feet to a wooden box, which has a cover tightly screwed on. Their task is to kneel down and carefully unscrew the top *without* jolting it. Why? There's a bomb inside, with an antimovement device. *SF Tomajczyk*

their job, whether to render a bomb harmless or actually disarming them when they're used as a bomb component. This is so important that within hours of a student's arrival, on the first day of training, he will find himself getting his first lecture on conventional explosives. By the third day, he is out on the range with explosives in hand. The fast-paced training only gets more intense from there.

In the second phase of the course, students learn all there is to know about fuzing mechanisms. A fuze is the device that causes the detonation of an explosive charge or bomb. From clocks to timers, they gain first-hand experience with mechanical, electrical and electronic fuzes.

The third phase is dedicated to bomb disposal equipment—how it is properly deployed and used, and what limitations each item has.

It is here that students play with robots, X-ray equipment, rigging gear, hand tools and disrupters. They also learn about the three types of bomb disposal trailers and how hazardous devices are safely transported to "cook-off points" where they are destroyed.

Bomb suit training is arguably the most entertaining portion of this phase. Students are introduced to several types of bomb suits and personal protection gear, which they all get to wear and try out. Many bomb suits weigh around 60 pounds and require the help of an assistant to put on.

One of the bomb suits used by HDS is the EOD-7B made by Med-Eng Systems, the undisputed leader in bomb suit development. When the 3/4-inch-thick ballistic glass plate is attached to the Kevlar helmet and put over your head, you can't help feeling like a deep sea diver. This is absolutely no place for someone who is claustrophobic. HDS instructors know this and watch students for any signs of panic. If a student gets nervous, he must learn to overcome his fear or be dropped from the course and forget about bomb disposal altogether.

Once a student is cocooned inside his bomb suit, he is taken outdoors to perform various drills. For example, he searches for and locates a wooden box that has its top tightly screwed in place. Kneeling down, the student unscrews the top and carefully removes it to reveal a fake bomb. If he has been too aggressive in removing the top, a mercury switch is tripped. A flashing light on the bomb indicates that he's dead. For the student who isn't expecting this, it can be a shocking revelation.

Another drill has the student lying on the ground, flat on his back. With 60 pounds encompassing you, getting up is not easy. It generally requires Frankenstein-like motions to rise and walk. Yet, bomb techs must learn how to do this in case they lose their balance or are bowled over by an explosion.

Although every FBI agent is trained to do crime scene work, his or her proficiency at gathering evidence is determined by the amount of field experience the agent possesses. "There's no question that somebody who does it all the time is better than somebody who does it intermittently," says HDS supervisor David Heaven.

Because of this, the FBI developed the concept of Evidence Response Teams (ERT), which specialize in collecting crime scene evidence. At least one eight-person ERT is assigned to each FBI field division. A typical team comprises a team leader, sketch artist, photographer, evidence custodian, and several evidence collectors. On the job, team members identify evidence, write tags, dust for fingerprints, and examine the crime scene while waiting for the artist, photographer and evidence custodian to document the items in place

before finally packaging them for transport to the FBI laboratory.

When necessary, other experts are added to the team. For instance, an odontologist is used to identify dental remains, and an entomologist can determine the time and place of a victim's death by looking at insect larvae.

Similarly, bomb technicians are brought in when explosive materials are found or if an actual explosion has taken place. The FBI has 90 to 100 bomb technicians on its staff. Since they know what a blast can do to various objects, they are skilled at identifying fragments, and they know what to collect. They are also helpful in figuring out what kind of explosive was used and how a bomb was built.

In recent years, FBI Evidence Response Teams were deployed to the Oklahoma City bombing and to the U.S. Embassy bombings in Kenya and Tanzania.

FBI Evidence Response Teams are responsible for gathering evidence at a crime scene, including terrorist bombings. This photo was taken at the 1996 Oklahoma City bombing. An ERT technician, dressed in white, is standing in the foreground. *Mike McGroarty*

They must also learn how to quickly remove the suit. Although it takes five minutes or longer to put on the armor, it can be taken off in about four seconds by simply pulling two rip cord handles and twisting the upper body to deposit the suit on the ground. This knowledge comes in handy if the suit ever catches fire or if the bomb tech has to sprint to safety to escape an explosion.

Besides learning how to work in a bomb suit, students also learn how to examine a bomb and its container for clues about how it is built and, more importantly, how it can be rendered safe. It is during this time period that the students spend nearly a week learning various removal and remote entry techniques. They also get their first look at military ordnance, which turns up more often than people realize.

Smoke on the Water, Fire in the Sky

The three training phases at HDS are usually covered in the first two weeks. The remainder of the Basic Course is dedicated to practical exercises, in which students practice disarming techniques. Much of the field work is done at a 350-acre site on Redstone along the Tennessee River. This forested area is enclosed by two fenced perimeters—an outer exclusion zone that keeps unwelcome guests and wandering cattle away, and an inner zone that encompasses 62 acres of firing ranges and test pits. There is also a small classroom, a mobile-trailer drug lab, a boobytrapped shack, and a bomb trailer or two at the range area.

For many students, this is the best part of HDS training. Without a doubt, it is also the most challenging, demanding their full attention and effort. Accidents do occur, although the instructors do everything they can to prevent them. The most serious injuries are generally minor scratches, cuts or bruises. But in 1987, a student was killed during training. David B. Pulling, a Delaware

Oops! He's dead. As indicated by the red light inside the box, this student was a bit too rough on the box while unscrewing its cover: He triggered the mercury switch. If this had been a real bomb, he'd be scattered all over Alabama right now. This is a lesson no student ever forgets. *SF Tomajczyk*

State Police officer, was setting up a disrupter to disable a bomb. It was an older piece of equipment, of a type no longer used by bomb technicians, that used a flashbulb initiator. Static electricity could easily set it off, and apparently that's exactly what happened. As Pulling approached the bomb with the disrupter cradled in his arms, a static charge built up and it went off prematurely. The recoil hit him squarely in the chest, essentially bursting his heart.

HDS has all students wear 100 percent cotton clothing to prevent static charge build-up. The school assigns one instructor to every four students and ensures that an ambulance is on-site, ready to respond to an emergency.

Reach out and touch someone . . . with a Hotstic retractable arm. There are times when a bomb tech really doesn't want to get close to a device. That's when this nifty tool comes in handy. It can pick up and retrieve items up to 15 feet away. As students are taught, distance is a bomb tech's best friend. *SF Tomajczyk*

As an example of the extreme care taken when working with live explosives, after setting up a demolition charge, students are marched 200 yards away from the test pit and accounted for before the charge is finally detonated. Protective glasses and ear plugs are required in these situations.

Training is made as realistic as possible. Students might respond to a fake 911 call and practice using a portable X-ray machine to examine a bomb hidden inside a briefcase. Once they figure out what they are dealing with, they either set up a disrupter to disarm the device where it sits, or set up rigging to drag the bomb and briefcase to a trailer, where it is then transported to a cook-off point and destroyed.

Much time is spent on pipe bombs, since it is the most common device encountered by civilian bomb technicians. Sophisticated bombs—those that use mercury switches or radio frequency detonators with exotic explosive charges—are rarely encountered. Why? Because acquiring the components is not easy,

and gaining the knowledge to safely build a complex bomb like this is even more difficult. More often than not, a bomber kills himself as he attempts to build a high-tech device. It is far easier (and safer) for a bomber to get his hands on a pipe and some black powder.

Although there are dozens of ways to rig a pipe bomb, it will always just be a pipe bomb. Taking this fact to heart, the students at HDS are taught how to use a disrupter to safely strip and disarm the bomb without setting it off. The key here is to make sure that the right type of disabling round is used and that the disrupter is set up properly. Pipe bomb training is done in test pits located in a remote area of the HDS field range.

Since the car bomb is popular among terrorists as a cheap, powerful and mobile weapon, HDS students also learn how to search vehicles for hidden explosives. In spite of their size, cars and trucks can be relatively difficult to work around. Imagine, for instance, trying to remove a bomb from the gas tank of a sports car. Do you flip the car on its side? Do you cut out the gas tank? Or do you just drag the entire vehicle off to a remote area and blow it up? There are no easy answers. If you end up deciding to disarm the bomb in place, then how do you position your disrupter so that it works properly in that cramped space?

Challenges like this are commonplace at HDS. Another field exercise that deserves mention is the so-called "marijuana field." Set in a wooded section of the range, this exercise has students conducting a long-distance approach to a drug-dealer's shack located in the middle of a field. First, the students have to navigate through the forest, which is bristling with booby traps. It's a demanding exercise since the dim light makes it difficult to see monofilament wire. This type of scenario pushes the extremes of the unforgiving conditions that the students may encounter when they return home.

HDS students learn how to operate a variety of robots, including this one, an Andros 6x6 robot. Command signals are sent to the robot via a tethered cable (rear). At the other end, several hundred feet away, a student controls the robot's actions by using joysticks. Closed-circuit video cameras on the robot send real-time images to a monitor that the student watches. The cameras become his eyes to what the robot sees and does. *SF Tomajczyk*

Interestingly, crazy environments such as this bring out the best in the students. They love the challenge, and they thrive on it.

At each training exercise, whether it's a car bomb or a clan lab, students practice their situation analysis skills, so that each action becomes second nature. They understand that every action follows a certain logic when it comes to approaching and disarming a device. It's not like television, where the hero crawls under a car and cuts the "right" wire at the last second.

A student finds himself asking questions like: What am I actually confronted with? Is the device life threatening? How large a safety perimeter should be established? What is the least amount of time I can spend on target? What render-safe procedure should I follow? What equipment do I need, and is it available? How long a soak time should I observe?

All of these questions need to be answered before any action is taken. "Everything is an unknown when you start," says Funderburg, adding that the ideal bomb tech has to take those unknowns and puzzle them out. "You want a person who is technically competent, who can remain calm under stress, and who can take charge and maintain control."

This means that a bomb tech must learn to ignore external forces, like impatient supervisors, local politicians and business owners who want to speed up the bomb disposal process. For instance, if a suspicious package is found inside a company, a bomb technician must not hasten his work just so the employees can go back inside for lunch. He has to be able to assert himself and do what's right . . . at the proper pace. His top priority is the safety of the public, followed by his own life. Property damage and public inconvenience should be a distant afterthought.

Room 402

Supplementing its field training exercises, HDS has several minilabs set up in two buildings. Each room simulates a different setting that a bomb tech could encounter on a call, including a hospital room, a radio station, a business office and a bar. Each has its own inherent problems. The students practice approaching and searching the rooms for a bomb, and then figuring out how to disarm the device or remove it.

In one case, the trainees are instructed to remove a pipe bomb from an office. When

The Hazardous Devices School is just one weapon in the FBI's war against bombers. The rest of the arsenal exists at the Bomb Data Center, which is located at FBI Headquarters in Washington, D.C. Under the control of Special Agent Steve Veyera, the Bomb Data Center is tasked with monitoring bombing trends, keeping bomb technicians abreast of new techniques, developing state-of-the-art counterbomb technologies, alerting bomb squads nationwide about threats, and helping bomb squads provide protection at public events.

The center accomplishes this in several ways. First, it shares technical information about bombs via bulletins and reports, and through the Law Enforcement On-Line web site. Much of this information is compiled from intelligence sources around the world. Second, the center oversees HDS and hosts proficiency training courses around America for bomb technicians. Third, it works closely with federal agencies to develop tools, sensors and equipment that can be used to defeat various types of bombs.

And last, the center offers its expertise and equipment to bomb squads who need assistance. For example, the center routinely sends its staff and equipment to major public events, such as the Goodwill Games and to the Republican and Democratic National Conventions. Their presence removes some of the pressure from local bomb squads, which still must respond to unrelated threats while the event is being held.

Concern is written all over this bomb tech's face. With terrorists making their bombs more sophisticated and deadly, he has to rely on information from the FBI's Bomb Data Center to keep up with developments in bomb-building techniques. *SF Tomajczyk*

Four sticks of dynamite, ready to go. A student has correctly wired and suspended the explosives in the center of a single-vent containment vessel. When they explode, the blast wave will be directed upwards. As evident from the blackened scars on the vessel's inner surface, this bomb trailer has been used before. *SF Tomajczyk*

they conduct a quick reconnaissance, the situation doesn't appear to be a problem. However, after sketching their plan out on paper, the trainees realize that getting the bomb to the trailer outside is going to require about 150 feet of rope and four break-away pulleys to drag the device out behind a door, through the office itself, down a narrow hallway, around a corner and through another room, then out the back door and across the lawn. The logistics are mind-boggling. Using patience and a bright, orange-colored traffic

cone to pad the pipe bomb from sharp knocks, they eventually manage to get the device safely inside the trailer.

While these individual labs are challenging, the biggest test is yet to come in Room 402. The hushed tones students use to speak of this room might lead you to believe that Darth Vader is lurking behind the steel door. Actually, it's more like something out of an Indiana Jones movie.

Room 402 is a virtual Fort Knox when it comes to booby traps. Comprised of three rooms, it is filled with just about every type of ingenious explosive device conceived by man. In fact, many of the bombs and booby traps found in the room mirror those actually encountered by bomb squads around the world.

In this training exercise, the students exchange their bomb suits for flak jackets, ballistic helmets and eye protection. They roll up their shirt sleeves so they can feel monofilament wires. Then they approach the room and carefully search it for booby traps. Few students make it past the front door.

HDS instructors have called upon all their years of experience to devise an unparalleled system of traps for this exercise. Pressure plates in the floor, invisible laser beams, monofilament trip wires, and even ingenious sonic triggers are found in Room 402. Disaster awaits a student at every turn. Doors explode when opened. Carpeted floors blow up when stepped on. Books fly apart when lifted or opened. And fish . . . well, it's astounding what the instructors can do with a fish.

As a student finishes searching one room, he must proceed to the next—and each room is seemingly more difficult than the previous one. If you panic, speed up or lose your concentration, you'll trigger a bomb. Not that it's necessarily bad to make a mistake and be "blown up." It's far better to make mistakes in Room 402 than out in the real world. In Room 402, the "explosions" can't kill you.

Life After HDS

As the Basic Course winds down and graduation day approaches, students spend a full day learning postblast investigation techniques (collecting evidence, setting up a crime scene, avoiding contamination). Their specialized knowledge of explosives and bomb components is invaluable to crime scene investigators, who rely on them to help them differentiate debris from actual bomb components.

"A bomb technician is more likely to know what the inside of a battery looks like when it's turned wrong-side-out by an explosion," says FBI agent David Heaven, who is in charge of HDS. "He's likely to know all the components of a watch or a clock and be able to recognize them, even if they're damaged. He knows what blast effects do to various objects. He knows what to collect."

To instill this knowledge, HDS has an extensive collection of batteries, clocks, watches, and fuzes from around the world. Many of these items have been blown up so the students can see what the surviving pieces look like. This helps them identify key markings that indicate the item was a bomb part.

The most important thing they learn during this session is how to avoid contaminating the crime scene. Since bomb techs work with explosives all their lives, they are the most "contaminated" people on Earth. On any given day you can find explosive residue under their fingernails, on their pocket knives or on the soles of their shoes. The Catch-22 of this, is that the bomb tech is needed on site to assist with the investigation. He plays a role in identifying fragments, determining how a bomb was assembled, where the materials came from, and how the bomb was placed on site. So care must be taken that he doesn't track in residue that will mess up the forensic investigation.

"He has to take exceptional measures to cover up and make sure he's clean," says

A bomb tech's worst nightmare is a clandestine drug lab filled with booby traps. In this 36-foot-long trailer, HDS teaches students how to search a clan lab for hazardous materials, explosives and trip wires. Obviously, this is not your typical kitchen. There are a lot of hazards here. If you were the bomb tech, where would *you* start?

Heaven. To achieve this, a bomb tech typically puts on booties, gloves and Tyvek coveralls before entering a bomb site.

Eventually, graduation day arrives. In return for their so-called "Bomb Degree," the students leave behind a plaque, which is hung in a long hallway in one of the classroom buildings. The plaque typically thanks—in poetic form—the HDS instructors for their efforts. For example:

HDTs are taught a lot of skills
To take apart a device before it kills.
But what it boils down to
So as to never to lose,
Is always remember to get, Le Fuze.

After graduation, each student maintains his proficiency by attending a mandatory Recertification Course at HDS every three years.

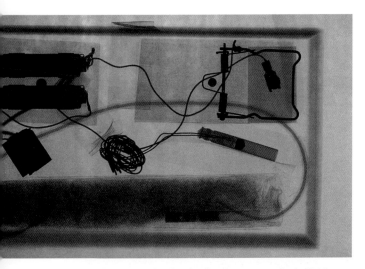

X-rays are great for figuring out how a terrorist built his bomb, but correctly interpreting the X-ray is another thing. This is a real-time X-ray taken of a bomb hidden inside a box. The explosive and blasting cap are located at the bottom of the picture, the trigger (a mousetrap) is at the upper right, and the power source (a battery) is in the upper left. The bomb is designed to blow up when a person opens the box, allowing the mousetrap to snap shut. Then BOOM! You're Swiss cheese. *FBI Hazardous Devices School*

Supplementing this is a national guideline for bomb techs to undergo 40 hours of explosives-related training each year. This is vital, since bombing trends and render-safe procedures constantly change.

"You never feel like you know that you've mastered this field," says Ray Funderburg. "Every day there's something to learn. It's not a matter that you'll learn something next month or next year . . . it's today."

On a day-to-day basis, bomb technicians rely on FBI special bulletins and Law Enforcement On-Line (LEO) to learn about new explosive devices, bombing incidents, and render-safe procedures. LEO, which is a secure web site dedicated for law enforcement use, features data sheets, a library of publications (e.g., technical bulletins, bomb schematics), and bulletin boards where bomb techs can post a question to the entire community ("Have you seen anything like this?"). LEO can also be used for research purposes. By hunting the database, a bomb tech can usually identify an unusual fuze or device.

A Bright Future

HDS is trying to prepare America's bomb squads for the threats of the twenty-first century. Arguably the school's most pressing agenda, is training bomb techs about chemical and biological terrorist attacks. David Heaven has established a schedule to assure that every bomb technician in America will receive intensive training on weapons of mass destruction. This course supplements the Department of Defense's efforts to get 120 cities up to speed on nuclear, biological and chemical threats.

"The bomb squad is absolutely a player in this game," stresses Heaven. "A weapon of mass destruction device may or may not have an explosive component, but it doesn't matter. If a briefcase is found, the bomb techs are going to be called in to examine it and X-ray it. So you've got to have them in there trained as part of the game."

The course teaches bomb technicians how to identify Weapons of Mass Destruction components and the emergency actions they can take to disarm the device or limit the number of casualties. The first step is to remain calm if they find something on an X-ray that resembles a chemical or biological agent. An X-ray showing a liquid-filled flask hidden inside a box doesn't mean that it's a nerve toxin or something worse. Rather, it's more likely to be gasoline, the incendiary liquid most often used by bombers.

"You've got to look at what's out there in reality," says Heaven. "For instance, there are incendiary bombs. Incendiary bombs throw gasoline, setting things on fire. *That's* what we see."

The bomb tech has to quickly evaluate the situation, making no assumptions. He must ask questions like, "Do I see nozzles or a solenoid switch to depress a nozzle?" and "Are there holes in the container to allow for the dispersion of a chemical or biological agent?" If the answer is yes, then he is likely dealing with a WMD device and needs to respond accordingly. Otherwise, he proceeds assuming that the device is conventional.

Heaven also intends to increase the number and diversity of courses being offered by HDS, which means the school must expand. To accomplish this, a $21.5 million training facility is being built at Redstone. It features classrooms, administrative areas, training labs, equipment areas and sites for disrupter use. There is also a mock city—complete with a strip mall, residential area, train station and a farmhouse—so that students can train in a realistic environment. Presently, the only other facility like this in the world is the Felix Centre in Great Britain.

Another endeavor is the creation of a technical database of terrorist groups. More specifically, a database that reveals bomb characteristics, unusual hazards, and trends on how bombs are being built and used. This could prove helpful to a technician who is handling a strange-looking device that is known to have been built by a specific terrorist or criminal group. Knowing how the terrorist group has assembled its bombs in the past (e.g., type of firing circuit, explosive load, container design) helps the bomb tech anticipate what he's up against and, more importantly, how to disarm it without endangering his own life.

Saving lives—those of the public and the bomb tech—is the underlying purpose of the Hazardous Devices School. Out in a remote corner of Redstone Arsenal, brave men and women from around America are taught how to thwart the evil of a terrorist bomb. It's not an easy task, but it is one that the instructors are committed to, knowing that the life of an innocent person can be safeguarded through a bomb technician's knowledge and skill.

Ray Funderburg summarizes the responsibility placed on HDS in this way: "We have to anticipate the possibilities, make people aware of the possibilities, and, in some cases, develop techniques for the possibilities."

However, like many others at HDS, Funderburg wishes the possibilities didn't exist in the first place.

This is a person that the FBI will never allow to retire. Why? Happy-go-lucky Stan Setzer makes all the bombs that HDS students must learn to disarm. Any time a new bomb-building method is discovered in the world, he's the one who recreates the device. There's no bomb he doesn't know how to make, which is why he's so valuable to the FBI. *SF Tomajczyk*

"Okay, you've got 10 minutes to identify these items," barks an instructor. He sweeps his hand over a grassy area littered with rockets, bombs and submunitions lying on the ground. "Determine if an item is indeed ordnance and, if so, what its nomenclature is, what safety precautions must be taken, what country it hails from, how it functions, and what the fuze condition is. And remember! Keep an eye out for copperheads! It's morning, and they're coming out to warm themselves in the sun. So don't go poking your hand where it doesn't belong."

The students, enlisted and officers alike, nod their heads and cautiously descend upon the weapons of war, keeping a wary eye out for signs of poisonous snakes. From an outsider's viewpoint, it appears they are more afraid of Mother Nature than the bombs they're inspecting. This becomes more apparent when they have to get down on their hands and knees to peer inside a 2.75-inch rocket launcher. They slowly inch forward, using flashlights to read the nomenclature stamped in the metal, and pencils to push aside tall grass, twigs and leaves that block their view

"Fear is a good thing in this business," chuckles one instructor. "You just have to make sure that it doesn't take control of you."

And learning how to manage that fear by relying on knowledge and skill is what Indian

> ## *"Wherever the bomb is, we have to get to it."*
>
> –Petty Officer Ken C. Anderson, U.S. Navy

Head, Maryland, is all about. For it is here, at the Naval School Explosive Ordnance Disposal (NAVSCOLEOD), where bomb technicians in the Army, Navy, Air Force and Marine Corps learn how to identify, render safe and dispose of military weapons and explosive devices, including nuclear warheads.

The 300-acre school is located on the banks of the Potomac River, some 25 miles south of Washington, D.C. It is a heavily wooded area of Maryland that is known for swamp-like conditions, complete with bloodthirsty insects and poisonous snakes. It is in this sweltering environment that young men and women learn everything there is to know about things that go "boom."

Two-Phase Training

The military's explosive ordnance disposal training program is broken into two distinct phases. Phase I is held at Eglin Air Force Base in the Florida panhandle. Lasting 12 weeks, the course teaches students the basic physical principles of explosives, rigging methods, basic demolition procedures, and ordnance transportation and storage. Students also learn how to correctly identify weapons, how to do reconnaissance on a bomb, and how to properly use EOD tools. Before the end of Phase I, everyone also undergoes chemical and biological warfare training—an increasingly important arena in

An EOD instructor prepares a contact mine for a training exercise. It will be tossed into a manmade pond where students will have to swim out to it and disarm it . . . without detonating it. A mission easier said than done, since the mine might have an acoustic sensor to "hear" the students' swimming toward it. *SF Tomajczyk*

A student takes a cautious peek at an aircraft rocket dispenser to see if there are any markings or features that will properly identify it. (He's also on the lookout for deadly snakes. The training area is loaded with copperheads.) In this business, you must absolutely know what you're up against before taking any action. *SF Tomajczyk*

today's world, where terrorists use Sarin gas or anthrax bomblets to do their deadly deeds.

From the sunny shores of Florida, the students travel north to Indian Head, where they spend 17 weeks going through Phase II. This intense training phase covers specific groups of ordnance. Students rotate through four divisions of the main school, beginning with ground ordnance, such as mines, proceeding through air ordnance, like missiles, then improvised explosive devices and, finally, ending with nuclear weapons. Classes are held 5 days a week for 8 hours a day, regardless of weather conditions. In the real world, EOD emergencies don't wait for a nice, sunny spring afternoon.

The only time training is delayed is when a severe thunderstorm hits the Indian Head area. Working on explosives when lightning fills the air with electricity is always a bad idea. When a storm approaches, (a regular summer occurrence) Indian Head's Automatic Lightning Warning System alerts EOD instructors of the danger by sending a message to a pager they wear. Training is also curtailed when the heat index soars to unhealthy levels in the summer.

During Phase II training, students are taught how to disarm land mines, booby traps, rockets, grenades, bombs, aircraft machine guns, guided missiles, submunitions, and projectiles. They also get an introduction to aircraft components that have explosive parts, but are not weapons, such as ejection seat systems and aerial flares.

Each of the four divisions has its own practical exercise area, where students practice on explosive devices. For instance, the Ground Ordnance Division has land mines and other hazards buried all over the place in a wooded area near the classrooms. Students are sent out to reconnoiter an area, locate and identify any ordnance, develop a render-safe procedure, and then dispose of the device(s). It is easier said than done.

For example, a land mine can be extremely difficult to spot, especially if it is buried in the shade of a tree with its wire-thin contact points hidden beneath some leaves. More than one EOD student has been "blown up" for moving too quickly in the woods, or for failing to remove his or her sunglasses.

Even if a mine is safely discovered, it still has to be removed and defuzed. That means checking for booby traps and then slowly . . . ever so slowly . . . digging up the mine with bare hands or nonmagnetic hand tools. Students are taught to clear all the way around the mine until they are certain that there are no booby traps or secondary

Roping a land mine takes a delicate touch, a skill this EOD technician possesses. Once the rope is in place, she'll back off quite a distance and slowly pull the mine out of the sand, to where it can then be safely disarmed. Women make up about 10 percent of the military EOD and civilian bomb disposal community in America. Note the nonmetallic probe to the left. It is held in the hand, palm-up. This allows the probe to slide free if it hits a mine. If it were held otherwise, the mine would likely explode from the strong contact. *SF Tomajczyk*

mines. Then, and only then, can they remove the mine and defuze it, using a rope to gently slide it out of the hole. From start to finish, it can take a student 1 hour to defuze just one mine.

At the Air Ordnance Division, students put on hard hats and explore the innards of nearly every type of aircraft in use with the U.S. military. Scattered over several acres of woodland are fighters (F-16 Fighting Falcon, F-15 Eagle, F/A-18 Hornet), bombers (FB-111 Aardvark), attack aircraft (A-10 Thunderbolt II) and helicopters (AH-1 Cobra). Students practice dealing with hung-up ordnance, such as a missile that didn't fire as it should have, jammed machine guns, and misbehaving submunition pods.

Since EOD technicians are often sent to crash sites, the Air Ordnance Division has made certain that its practical exercise area has examples of destroyed aircraft, including F-4 Phantom II fighters, which were used during the Vietnam conflict and are still found today in the jungles of Southeast Asia. To make things realistic, many of the planes' parts are positioned upside-down and partly buried into the earth, just as they would be if the plane had actually crashed. The same holds true for unexploded ordnance. Bombs, aircraft submunitions, rockets and missiles stick out of the dirt all over the place, giving the landscape a stubbled "5 o'clock shadow" appearance. Students hone their skills here by dealing with the carefully manufactured chaos of buried hazards.

Each of the four divisions ends its training course with several days of final exams, in which students are graded on their ability to safely approach, identify, render safe and dispose of a piece of ordnance, either U.S. or foreign made. Most of these tests have a 90-minute time limit and are quite intense. If a student fails, he is retested the next day. If he fails again, he then goes before an Academic Review Board, which makes a recommendation to the Commanding Officer whether or not he should be removed from EOD training altogether.

Students can flunk a test for failing to recognize a booby trap, for violating a safety precaution, for using an incorrect render-safe procedure, or for not completing a procedure properly. Safety is paramount in this field, and the Academic Review Board has no sympathy for would-be EOD techs who are incompetent or reckless.

Upon successfully completing a division, the group of 25 or so students then moves on to the next, until all four are completed. At the end of Phase II training, Army, Air Force and Marine Corps students proudly pin on their "crab," the insignia of an EOD technician, and return to their units or continue with additional training courses. At this point, attrition will have taken its toll. For example, the Army typically loses 31 percent of its students during Phase I and 20 percent of the remainder during Phase II. Most of the other services don't fare any better. EOD training is

A student checks a rocket with a dental mirror and pencil to ensure that the motors have completely burned. He uses a pencil since it is non-sparking. If any propellant is still in the chamber, a spark could cause an unexpected "burn" or explosion. *Joyce Welch*

extremely tough, both mentally and physically. As instructor Chief Thomas Foster, U.S. Navy, says, "If you're not at 105 or 110 percent performance here, you're in trouble."

Only the Navy does better. Its attrition rate at NAVSCOLEOD is 8 percent during Phase I and 9.4 percent during Phase II, but that's because their students have gone through the equally intense Navy Dive School prior to attending Indian Head. Those who are likely to drop out of the EOD program usually do so long before heading for NAVSCOLEOD.

Underwater Training

Navy EOD students attend a fifth division, the Underwater Ordnance Division, for an additional 13 weeks of training. It is here they learn about mines, torpedoes, underwater tools, and disabling techniques. This school is located near the Potomac River in a remote part of Indian Head known as Area 8.

The division's mascot is a black cat named Eightball. He wears a miniature version of the unlucky billiard ball on his collar and has full run of the facility, which he uses to watch the students with a critical eye as they go about their training. Appropriately, the school's unofficial slogan is, "Scratch, and you lose," a metaphor whose double meaning is not lost on anyone.

At the Underwater Ordnance Division, students start off with a refresher course on how to properly use the Navy's Mark 16 Underwater Breathing Apparatus. This mixed-gas rebreather system produces no bubbles, is designed to defeat mines or torpedoes equipped with acoustic sensors. The Mark 16 costs upward of $40,000 and can be used for up to 8 hours before having to be recharged, depending on the diver's depth and how hard he is working.

Students initially practice underwater search techniques in an indoor pool, which is 24-feet deep with clear visibility, although the

EOD techs are a superstitious lot, and rightly so. What can go wrong, often does. Which is why students avoid "Murphy" (in ball cap above) like the plague during their training at the Ground Ordnance Division. They appease him with various offerings so he won't cause them to flunk out of the class. Instructors take a different approach. They enjoy partying with Murphy out on the town. *SF Tomajczyk*

instructors like to turn off all the lights to force the divers to go through procedures in darkness. Eventually the class graduates to working in the murky Potomac and Patuxent rivers. Both waterways are a good place for the students to learn how to identify objects by touch and how to recover ordnance buried in the deep ooze of the river bottom.

43

"Flipper" Joins the Navy

The Navy, like other military branches and law enforcement agencies, uses dogs as part of its counter-bomb efforts. But the Navy also has another tool when it comes to finding underwater ordnance underwater—dolphins and sea lions. Officially known as the Marine Mammal Program, the Naval Ocean Systems Center in San Diego, California, has studied dolphins, sea lions and whales for decades to better understand echolocation and hydrodynamics.

Dolphins, for instance, have been used for surveillance and underwater demolition operations, as well as to conduct combat patrols, searching out enemy frogmen. Dolphins were sent to the Persian Gulf in the 1980s to do security patrols around allied naval vessels. And, until recently, dolphins patrolled nuclear submarine bases at Bangor, Washington, and Kings Bay, Georgia. They have since been replaced by the Navy Waterside Security System and SCOUT, a high-tech underwater intruder sensor system.

Originally, the Navy had about 100 dolphins in its program. But 30 of the animals were retired in 1994 and sent to marine parks around the nation. The reason for the downsizing was attributed to the end of the Cold War and the high cost of maintaining them.

The remaining dolphins are used to locate mines. A marker device, which slides over the dolphin's nose, is placed close to any mine the dolphin encounters. The marker then separates into two pieces—one, an anchoring device that remains on the bottom near the mine and another that floats to the surface. An EOD diver then swims down, following the line from the float to the anchor to identify and, if necessary, disarm the mine.

As for sea lions, they are used to locate and recover missiles, torpedoes and mines that have been used in tests. In 1975, the "Quick Find" demonstration program proved that sea lions could indeed be trained to find instrumented ordnance, thereby saving money on replacements.

"Sea lions are outstanding for recovery of test mines," says Petty Officer Ken Anderson, a NAVSCOLEOD instructor who has worked with marine mammals. "They can recover mines in a field a lot faster than

The Navy uses mammals, like this dolphin, to locate mines underwater. The dolphin places the marker near a mine; the marker separates, with one part floating to the surface, trailing a line behind it. Navy EOD divers then swim down, following the line to the mine, and dearm it. *U.S. Navy*

divers. With a lot of mines to recover, you can burn out your divers pretty fast, whereas these animals won't burn out. As long as they're getting fish, they're happy."

To recover a missile, the sea lion is sent over the side of the boat to locate it underwater. The sea lion returns and presses its nose against a rubber pad after it hears the missile's salt water-activated acoustic "pinger." A bite plate, which is a flat piece of metal with a neoprene covering, is then placed in the sea lion's mouth. As she swims down to the object, the line attached to the bite plate is spooled out from the boat. The sea lion attaches the recovery device to the missile, releases the bite plate, and then returns to the surface where it receives some fish as a reward. A floating marker is then attached to the line so that a recovery vessel can find the missile later. It is usually raised to the surface by a gas bag inflated by a hydrazine gas generator. This system can recover objects to a depth of 500 feet. Today, the Navy maintains a sea lion detachment at both San Diego, California, and Charleston, South Carolina.

The Navy, as part of its "Deep Ops" program, has also trained a pilot whale, two killer whales and an unknown number of Beluga whales to recover objects from great depths. Using a device similar to that used by sea lions, the pilot whale was able to successfully recover a torpedo from a depth of 1,654 feet.

Make a mistake while working on a mine, and you'll quickly know it. Each piece of ordnance is wired to 1/4-pound of TNT hidden in a nearby water hole. When a student makes the wrong move, the TNT explodes, showering him in muddy water and embarrassment. It's a reminder that he needs to be more careful in the future *SF Tomajczyk*

But not all underwater ordnance training is done underwater: The most challenging training takes place in the woods and marshlands surrounding Area 8. Understanding that mines and torpedoes are found washed up on beaches around the world, or are towed ashore to be disabled by EOD techs on land, the division has deliberately littered its grounds with inert ordnance. You'll find contact mines sitting in a shallow stream in the woods, torpedoes embedded in mud holes, and influence mines stuck in the wetland muck of Mattawoman Creek. No matter what the training situation is, it's guaranteed to be a wet, muddy and miserable experience. That's because the Navy is always called upon to respond to any ordnance found in the water. So the training at Area 8 mirrors what the students can expect to deal with in the real world. (There is a joke among Navy EOD techs that Army and Air Force personnel intentionally toss ordnance found on land into any nearby water, even if it's a puddle, just so they won't have to deal with it.)

Although the students dealt with a similar field exercise area at the Ground Ordnance Division, Area 8 adds a new twist—high explosives. Every practice mine and torpedo is wired to a quarter-pound of TNT. If a student makes a mistake while completing a disarming exercise, the explosive charge detonates about 75-feet away from him. The TNT is always hidden in a deep puddle of water. When it explodes, not only does everyone nearby hear it, but they also see a column of water shooting 60 feet into the air. For the student who made the mistake and is now mud soaked, this embarrassing moment reinforces the need to be more careful in the future. If he had been performing a real EOD mission, his sloppiness would have just cost him his life.

"We want the students to make all their mistakes here, not out in the real world," says NAVSCOLEOD instructor Petty Officer Ken Anderson. "That's why we push them so hard. We don't want them to become a casualty."

It's also why there is one instructor for every five students. They want to make sure that the students are well supervised so they not only do a procedure correctly, but so they don't get injured while they learn. Because of this monitoring system, most of the injuries

Why won't this %$#! thing budge? A lieutenant tries to remotely open up a torpedo warhead that is located in the woods about 300 feet away. The rope is attached to the warhead by a series of pulleys. It takes a lot of muscle work and precision to pop the torpedo housing off. Students are given 3 hours to accomplish this task, one of several tests they must pass. This lieutenant failed on this particular attempt. He tripped the 1/4-pound TNT charge. *SF Tomajczyk*

students sustain are minor in nature, such as cuts, bruises and sprains. But that doesn't mean more serious injuries can't occur. They do from time to time, and usually when diving underwater.

"Most diving-related injuries are shallow water injuries," explains Anderson. "That's because the greatest change in atmospheric pressure is from the surface down to 33 feet."

To illustrate this, he says, if you took a cup and inverted it, and then dove down to 33 feet underwater, you would discover that the cup would contain only half the air it had at the surface. That's because the air has been compressed into half the space. If you continued swimming down another 33 feet, the air would only compress another quarter. Hence, the greatest pressure change is in the first 33 feet from the surface.

This compression has a similar effect on the gases present in a diver's lungs and bloodstream. Injury can occur when a diver ascends to the surface after being underwater for even a short period of time. For example, if he holds his breath while surfacing, the air in his lungs will overexpand, rupturing lung tissue and blood vessels. Likewise, if a diver doesn't decompress properly, taking breaks as he surfaces, gas bubbles in his bloodstream can get so large that they become trapped, causing a painful and crippling condition called nitrogen narcosis (better known as "the bends").

Diving-related injuries like these can be life threatening, which is why the Navy maintains hyperbaric decompression chambers throughout its fleets. At Indian Head, the hyperbaric chamber contains two beds and enough medical equipment to save a diver's life.

You gotta love the water if you want to be a Navy EOD technician . . . even if it's slimy green water. As they say in this business, you don't have to like it, you just have to do it. *SF Tomajczyk*

If a diver surfaces complaining of severe joint pain, for instance, the medical officer rushes him to a hyperbaric chamber for treatment. Once sealed inside (wearing only 100 percent cotton clothing or nothing at all), the diver is "pressed." In other words, the pressure inside the chamber is increased to match the same pressure he experienced while diving. Then, over a period of hours or days, depending on the severity of the illness, he is slowly decompressed to one atmosphere—the pressure found at sea level.

All Navy EOD students are trained in diving medicine and emergencies. It's important to know how to deal with a crisis when you're 130 feet below the ocean's surface in silty darkness, whether it's a shark attack, the bends, or an empty air tank.

By the time the students finally pin their "crab" insignia on their chest, nearly a year has passed since they first started on their journey to become an EOD technician. It's been 42 weeks of intense training that has taught them skills as uncommon as those of the elite Navy SEALs and as mentally demanding as the Navy's nuclear submarine force.

The World of Navy EOD

The Navy has two EOD Groups: Group 1 is headquartered in San Diego, California, and Group 2 is based out of Little Creek, Virginia. Each group comprises three Mobile Units which, in turn, are made up of 10 to 15 individual detachments. An average detachment has eight enlisted men and two officers, usually lieutenants. The detachments support the efforts of the surface fleet and the mine countermeasures community.

For example, a detachment is routinely based on an aircraft carrier to address the needs of the entire battle group. The EOD technicians deal not only with aircraft ordnance, such as a jammed gun or a misfired aerial flare, but also with any mines that the ships encounter.

A large percentage of Navy EOD technicians are parachute qualified and have received training in fast-roping and helo-casting, insertion techniques generally reserved for SEALs. That's because EOD techs have to go where the bombs are.

"We dive to get to the bomb, we jump to get to the bomb, or we helo-cast to get to a floater," says Anderson. "Wherever the bomb is, we use whatever means necessary to accomplish our mission."

In addition to supporting battle groups at sea, bomb technicians also support elite tactical teams of all the armed services when they deploy on a mission. This includes the Force Recon, Army Rangers, Navy SEALs and the counterterrorist unit DevGru (formerly, SEAL Team 6). The EOD techs assist in shallow water reconnaissance for mines and they follow an assault to disarm explosives and booby traps.

The insignia of a "Master Blaster," the highest trained EOD technician in the military, and one of the most difficult ratings to acquire. *SF Tomajczyk*

Field activities, such as fast-roping from a helicopter onto a pitching ship's deck in a storm, rather than disarming a bomb, tend to make EOD techs nervous. "Most ordnance, as long as you don't kick it or fool with it too much, you can pretty much do everything you need to do and still render it safe," Anderson says. "We attack the fuze, not the bomb. We never cut a wire unless we know what it does, unlike what you see in the movies."

He points out that training and insertion techniques, like parachuting and diving, kill or injure more bomb techs than those who are hurt disarming bombs. Anderson recounts breaking a foot during one parachute drop, when he made an error in landing, and having to cut away his main chute on another jump. In the latter incident, his parachute lines got tangled over the canopy. He had to cut it away and then rely on his reserve chute to safely make it to the ground.

Parachuting and helo-casting aside, about the only other thing in the EOD field that makes bomb techs nervous, is a type of ordnance that is called "alive." An "alive" device is equipped with one or more sensors that can passively sense, watch and track an EOD tech long before he realizes that it's even there. If a tech gets too close without spotting it or if he fails to correctly identify it from a safe distance, he'll likely be killed when the ordnance explodes as he approaches. EOD techs consider these devices to be extremely hazardous (a.k.a. "bad juju") and do all they can to avoid walking up on them.

This is one reason why EOD techs have been trained to identify ordnance from a distance. Using binoculars, a good tech can correctly ID a device simply by its size and shape. If not, he can narrow down the possibilities to general categories, such as a projectile, mine or torpedo. Then, using a CD-ROM computer database, which contains information on all known ordnance in the world, he can enter key words and search for possible matches. For example, a bomb tech can enter basic descriptive characteristics like:

Item: Torpedo
Length: 12 feet
Diameter: 21 inches
Color: Blue-gray
Markings: English

Within seconds he will be able to narrow the search to two or three possibilities, or even just one. Based on that information, he then knows what he's dealing with and can follow the correct render-safe procedure to disarm the device.

Master Blaster

Just because an EOD technician has successfully completed NAVSCOLEOD, it doesn't mean that his formal training has ended. His days of education continue as long as new ordnance is being developed, which is

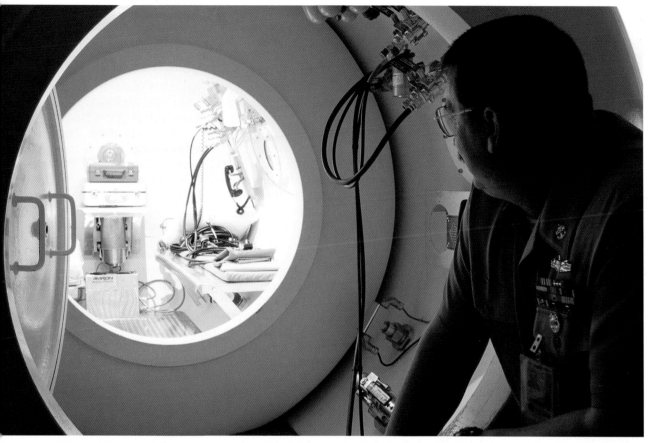

This is a tube no EOD diver ever wants to see. That's because it's a hyperbaric chamber. It's used to treat divers for the bends and other pressure-related ailments. This particular chamber is equipped to handle the medical needs of two divers. *SF Tomajczyk*

going on all the time, and as older, less-known ordnance is routinely dug up. Although much of a bomb tech's education is done on the job, he does receive more structured training through seminars hosted at Indian Head and elsewhere.

In the military, there are three levels of EOD techs: Basic, Senior and Master. Each service has its own requirements as to how its personnel achieve these levels. The Master EOD level is the rating that most technicians strive for, desiring to be known as a "Master Blaster." To achieve this distinction means that you are capable of running an entire EOD operation from start to finish.

To attain the Master EOD qualification in the Navy is tough—two years of training and experience stand between Basic and Senior rankings, and 3 years between Senior and Master. And there are absolutely no guarantees that you'll make it just by putting in your time.

"You're not guaranteed to move up the ladder," says Petty Officer Anderson, who is working toward his Master badge. "You have to prove that you're capable of doing the job."

The final step to becoming a Navy Master Blaster is to survive a 3-hour oral review board, which is composed of several experienced Master EOD techs. They collectively determine if a candidate is qualified and ready to move up to their ranks. During the interview, the candidate is posed with various scenarios and asked how he would deal with them. The scenarios are complicated, often involving multiple explosives and ordnance, and often located in challenging environments, like the Arctic or the tropics.

For example, a candidate may be asked to dispose of World War II-vintage ordnance uncovered on the Pacific island of Okinawa. How is he going to do it? The candidate must then explain in detail every step, from start to finish, that he would take to resolve the issue: orders and messages that would be given, support equipment and transportation that would be taken, food and supplies that would be needed, explosives that would be required for countercharges, etc. It is a detailed litany, in which the candidate must not overlook anything. If he does, the board can recommend to the Commanding Officer that he not pass.

For this reason, the Master EOD Technician is highly respected within the EOD community. People know that a Master Blaster has endured a tremendous amount of advanced training and is more than worthy of wearing the laurel-encircled star over his "crab" insignia.

In the Navy, a third of its 800 EOD technicians are Master Blasters. They have served in all positions of an EOD detachment, and have successfully attended advanced courses in foreign ordnance, advanced access and disablement, and EOD management and technology. Some of these courses are offered by the Department of Energy, FBI, and Department of Defense. They have also learned combat skills such as low intensity conflict and patrolling techniques so they can operate skillfully in a hot war zone.

A New EOD School

In 1998, NAVSCOLEOD began relocating its Indian Head facility to Eglin Air Force Base in Florida. This will consolidate Phase I and Phase II training at one central location. The move saves money and gives students better training facilities than those historically offered at Indian Head. For example, all the classrooms, which are now housed in a main building at Eglin instead of at four different complexes, feature air conditioning, new computers and audio-visual equipment.

Additionally, the students are able to work with larger explosive charges. At Indian Head's Stump Neck range, they were limited to 20-pound shots. But now, at Eglin's test ranges, they can work with explosives of up to 1,000 pounds. This means that aircraft bombs and underwater mines can be blown up with actual countercharges, giving students a better feel for how to do a render-safe procedure, rather than having to wait for an actual deployment to find out.

At Eglin, NAVSCOLEOD has situated its four divisions at Range 51, a huge, triangular-shaped property that encompasses some 3,000 acres. All the command post facilities are located here, along with the classrooms. Two additional ranges, 52W and 52N, are available for actual demolition procedures. Students are able to go down into a hole, pack some C-4 around a Mark 80 series bomb, and then blow it in place. They can witness the detonation from the safety of a nearby underground bunker, which has mirrors suspended overhead facing the blast area. By looking up at the mirrors, the students watch the explosion while avoiding fragments and the blast wave. It is an excellent training tool.

Navy EOD divers generally work in water depths up to 130 feet. These two divers are working on a contact mine. Note the absence of bubbles. That's because they're wearing the Mark 16 Underwater Breathing Apparatus, a rebreather system that eliminates noisy bubbles. *U.S. Navy*

Another benefit of moving NAVSCOLEOD to Eglin, is one of convenience. Panama City, home of the Navy's Dive School, is an hour away. Likewise, follow-on schools for the other services are much closer to Eglin than to Indian Head. For instance, Army EOD techs are routinely sent to Redstone Arsenal in Huntsville, Alabama, for four weeks of training after getting their "crab." Huntsville is a few hours drive due north of Eglin.

As NAVSCOLEOD consolidates itself for the future, it is also preparing for the next wave of explosive ordnance work. The number of bombings around the world has risen, and military EOD technicians are finding themselves in greater demand than ever before. More threats are being made not only against military bases but also against personnel. The June 1996 bombing of Khobar Towers in Saudi Arabia illustrates this.

Military EOD techs are also finding themselves being called overseas to help clear minefields in Bosnia and other parts of the world as part of peacekeeping missions. And they are also being used more here at home, assisting federal agencies in sweeping for improvised explosives at special events, like the G-7 Economic Summit and major sporting events.

As the demand for military EOD technicians increases, so will the training pace at NAVSCOLEOD. Presently, there are simply not enough EOD techs in the military to respond to every request that comes in. There are only about 3,000 men and women trained to respond to worldwide de-mining efforts and ordnance-related missions. Clearly, numbers like this suggest a daunting task, but the EOD technicians are willing to do their best in spite of it. They know that lives are at stake . . . and so they willingly walk toward a bomb while everyone else runs away. They are the true heroes in this world.

It was the evening of December 17, 1995, eight months after the Oklahoma City bombing. Two men drove into the parking lot at the Internal Revenue Service building in Reno, Nevada, and unhooked a dolly that had a 30-gallon plastic drum wired to it. Inside the container was 100 pounds of ANFO, a high-explosive mixture made from ammonium nitrate fertilizer and fuel oil . . . the same deadly ingredients used in the blast at the Alfred P. Murrah Federal Building, which killed 168 people. The men hid the bomb behind a parked car, lit the three-foot-long fuse, and then sped off.

Fortunately, the bomb didn't explode. The next morning, an IRS employee discovered the container and called police. Within minutes, the building and surrounding area was evacuated and a bomb squad was brought in to handle the device. A brief investigation resulted in the arrest 11 days later of Ellis Edward Hurst, 52, and Joseph Martin Bailie, 40. They were charged with attempted destruction of a government building and the use of a destructive device. Bailie, a tax protester who had a personal gripe with the IRS, was subsequently sentenced to 36 years in prison.

Normally, these facts are what people would read in their newspapers and hear on television at night, then the story would fade away. There is more to this case—call it "The ATF Story." In order to prove that the container was indeed a destructive device, as outlined by federal law, the ATF had to dismantle it and take samples of the bomb components for analysis. That meant that an Explosives Enforcement Officer (EEO), the ATF's equivalent of a bomb technician, had to walk up to the 100-pound bomb and carefully take it apart.

This kind of evidence gathering is a very dangerous and little-known facet of bomb disposal. Yet it happens all the time and it is responsible for the prosecution of would-be bombers.

"We are the bomb experts."

Art Resnick, Program Manager, ATF

Explosives Technology Branch

Although the Bureau of Alcohol, Tobacco and Firearms has been known by many official-sounding names, it can trace its heritage back to 1863, when Congress authorized hiring three detectives to help enforce tax laws. Over the following century, the agency became progressively involved in the regulation and taxation of alcoholic beverages, tobacco products and the firearms industry. It wasn't until the late 1960s—with the passage of the 1968 Gun Control Act and the 1970 Organized Crime Control Act—that the ATF finally entered the bomb business.

The Explosives Technology Branch (ETB) is the ATF's bomb squad. It is comprised of 23 Explosives Enforcement Officers, all of whom have previous experience as bomb techs with either the military or a law enforcement agency. In fact, most of the EEOs have 20 to 25 years of experience handling explosive devices and rendering them safe.

The ATF investigates bombings and arson incidents. Here, an ATF agent collects evidence to send to the laboratory for analysis. It is stored in a sterile metal container. *Bureau of Alcohol, Tobacco & Firearms*

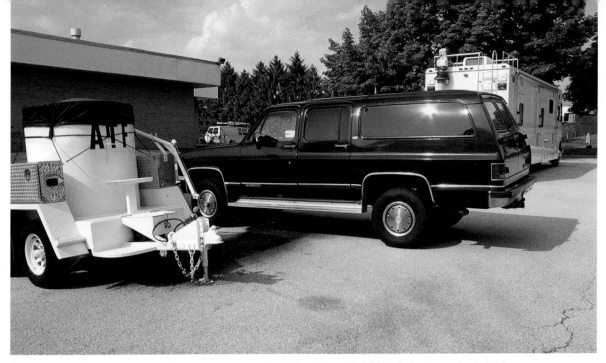

The ATF's Explosives Enforcement Officers are fully equipped "bomb squads." This photo shows the Suburban response vehicle they use (it is equipped with a bomb suit, disrupter, X-ray system, counter-charge explosives and hand tools), along with a single-vent containment vessel. In the background is the ATF's mobile command post. *SF Tomajczyk*

The EEOs provide technical assistance to bomb squads around the nation, respond to requests for bomb disposal assistance, help investigate bomb scenes, reconstruct explosive devices based on fragments and components found at the scene, disassemble and render safe live devices for evidentiary purposes, and give expert witness testimony in court on whether or not an item is a destructive device. (It is interesting to note that EEOs are the only technicians in America who have the statutory authority to determine if something is indeed an explosive device under federal law.) They also participate on the National Response Team (NRT) and accompany ATF agents on search warrants to handle booby traps or any bombs that are found.

Although the Explosive Technology Branch is located at ATF headquarters in Washington, D.C., it has satellite offices around the country, each staffed by four to five EEOs who respond to incidents in a certain geographic area. For instance, the Walnut Creek, California, office has five bomb techs who cover everything west of the Rocky Mountains. The Chicago office covers the Midwest; the Atlanta office handles the Southeast and Texas. The Rockville, Maryland, office covers New England and the Atlantic seaboard as far south as the North Carolina border.

Every bomb tech has his own response vehicle, a Chevy Suburban or Ford van, which is equipped with an EOD-7B bomb suit, a search suit, a PAN disrupter, grenade and pipe bomb spin-out tools, basic hand tools, a digital camera, a phone, a radio, and a portable X-ray system. They also carry small amounts of explosives for countercharge purposes.

"Anything you could imagine a bomb tech would need or want, we've got on our truck," says David S. Shatzer, a former Army

ATF Explosives Enforcement Officers are trained to handle and render safe hazardous devices. Many of them have 15 to 25 years of experience in bomb disposal. Here, an EEO examines the underside of a vehicle for a bomb. *Bureau of Alcohol, Tobacco & Firearms*

EOD technician who has been an ATF bomb tech for 10 years. "We're as well equipped as any major city bomb squad. We have everything we need to do anything out of that truck—except for nuclear, biological or chemical incidents of course."

Supplementing the response vehicle, every ETB satellite office is also equipped with a real-time X-ray system, a single-vented bomb trailer, a TR-2000 robot and night-vision devices that can be used by the bomb techs when necessary.

With this capability, an ATF bomb tech can generally be anywhere in the continental United States with a fully equipped truck in 12 to 15 hours.

Crimes of Passion

Although the FBI is the lead agency in matters involving terrorist bombings, 98 percent of the bombings in the United States do not involve terrorists. These other cases, and there are many, are all handled by the ATF. Between 1991 and 1995, for example, there were 8,567 incidents involving explosives, 2,078 attempted bombings, and 2,468 fire bombings resulting in arson. In 1997 alone, the ATF bomb techs participated in more than 300 bombing investigations and defuzed bombs in many of these, often involving multiple explosive devices and booby traps. It is an understatement to say that ATF's bomb techs are busy.

Here is a sampling of some of the bombings that the ATF has responded to. As you'll quickly note, the majority stem from revenge or jealousy:

- In Florida, a bomb was discovered strapped to the underside of a vehicle. The bomb consisted of two steel pipes with end caps bound together by duct tape, a servomotor, various wires, more than a pound of Pyrodex, several batteries and a light bulb initiator. The ATF and Palm Beach County Sheriff's Office eventually determined that the bomb was built by the ex-husband of the victim's wife. The bomber was angry that his wife had divorced him and remarried. He had made numerous threats against the new husband. Fortunately the bomb did not explode.

- In Maryland, a man used a bomb to kill his wife, children and himself in a murder/suicide plot, which was later revealed in letters he mailed to his parents. The explosion took place in the parking lot of a shopping center in suburban Baltimore. He had stolen some high explosives, then lured his estranged wife and children into the vehicle and detonated the bomb.

- In Pennsylvania, a husband and wife were sentenced to 7 to 15 years in prison for their roles in a pipe bombing. The victim had been romantically involved with the

It takes science to link a bomber with a bomb and then put him behind bars. That's where the ATF's National Forensic Laboratories enter the picture. The agency's laboratory system is composed of the National Laboratory Center (NLC) in Rockville, Maryland, and two regional labs located in Atlanta and near San Francisco. They hold the distinction of being the first federal laboratories to be accredited by the American Society of Crime Laboratory Directors. Only the Drug Enforcement Administration and U.S. Fish & Wildlife Service have since received that accreditation for their scientific facilities—as of this writing, the FBI has not.

In any given year, these labs process evidence from 500 to 700 bombing cases, one of the largest case loads of any agency in the world. This fact is even more amazing when you learn that the ATF labs have only about 80 technicians involved in forensic science.

After a bomb explodes, the debris and evidence are shipped in huge cartons to the lab. The forensic chemists go through the "trash"—which is often covered in the blood of the injured and the dead—separating out bomb components and fragments. They also search for and identify any explosive residue that is present. If a bomb signature exists, they are expected to notice it and/or hunt for it.

Doing this is easier said than done. An ATF chemist must be able to distinguish "normal" items like car wiring from the wiring used in a bomb. He is also expected to correctly identify electronic parts and circuit boards used in a radio-controlled bomb. The same holds true for correctly identifying the manufacturer of a smokeless powder used in a pipe bomb.

To do this, the forensic chemist relies not only on experience, but also on high-tech analytical equipment. This can include scanning electron microscopes to identify the elemental composition of wires or paint chips; X-ray diffractors to analyze powders and residues; and gas chromatographs to identify explosive compounds.

Also at the chemist's disposal are huge in-house collections of bomb components and explosives, which he can match his evidence against. The sample bomb components, known as exemplars, are housed in a room that is literally lined with floor-to-ceiling drawers. Here you'll find every battery known to mankind, as well as clocks, timers, aerial flares, pipe nipples, switches, blasting caps, gas cylinders, radio control devices, detonation cord, etc.

Another unique forensic weapon is a practice known as "toolmarking." The tools that a bomber uses to construct a device typically leave tell-tale marks behind. For instance, tightening the cap on a pipe bomb usually requires a wrench of some sort. By examining the cap, the chemist can figure out what type and what size wrench was used, how large the teeth were, etc. Knowing this can help ATF investigators identify the tool when conducting a search at a suspect's home or business.

"We've come up with some novel ways of tying the bomber to the bomb through the recovery of his tools," says Richard Strobel, a forensic chemist at the National Laboratory Center. He added that the lab has matched knives to a piece of plastic cut out for a bomb, wire cutters to the wiring, and screwdrivers to screw heads.

In 1995, the lab started using the EGIS Explosive Detector. This sensor, which resembles a hand-held Dustbuster-like vacuum, is used at postblast scenes to identify explosive residues. A technician "vacuums" a suspected area and then inserts the collection cartridge into a box-shaped, high-speed gas chromatograph, which searches for nitrogen–oxygen chemical bonds unique to certain explosives. Although the chromatograph weighs 400-pounds, it can be broken into two parts and placed in a vehicle for transport to a bomb scene. Technicians can have it up and running, and identifying chemical residues within an hour.

The EGIS detector was used in the Oklahoma City bombing, as well as at the abortion clinic blast in Birmingham. In the latter event, the EGIS

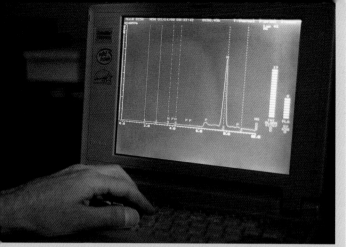

By using an EGIS detector to collect fumes at a bombing and then analyzing them with a high-speed gas chromatograph, ATF forensic chemists can determine what explosives were used at a bomb scene. The computer display in this photo reveals the presence of TNT in the sample (red bar at right). The ATF has relied on high technology like this to solve many bombings across the country. *SF Tomajczyk*

was driven down and set up in a local laboratory. Within hours, it had identified the type of explosive used in the bomb. Several days later, the instrument was driven to Murphy, North Carolina, where bombing suspect Eric Rudolph was believed to be hiding. Explosive detection dogs pinpointed the presence of bomb residue on a forest trail, which was confirmed by EGIS.

To enhance its bomb investigations, the lab recently acquired a Rapid Response Laboratory. It is essentially an 18-foot trailer that is towed by a Chevy Suburban to the bomb scene. The unit is designed so that it can be outfitted with whatever equipment is needed for a particular investigation. The inside area is divided into two sections: a 6-foot-long general work and examination area (which is equipped with a comparison microscope, an image enhancement system, telephones, and modem connections for computers), and a 12-foot-long work area for explosive and fire debris analysis.

The Rapid Response Lab is based in the Washington, D.C., metropolitan area, and is available to provide worldwide assistance to law enforcement. The ATF intends to purchase two additional mobile labs, which will be stationed at its two regional laboratories.

wife. After a dispute with her lover, she had urged her husband to place a pipe bomb in the victim's car. The explosion severely injured the man, who spent five months in the hospital.

• In Utica, New York, a pipe bomb exploded under a car. Fortunately, the owner was not hurt. The suspect was the ex-boyfriend of the victim's girlfriend. When confronted by the ATF and Utica Police, the suspect admitted that he had indeed built the bomb and placed it under the vehicle. His motive was jealousy.

To take some of the work load off bomb techs' shoulders, the ATF has trained some 300 agents as Certified Explosives Specialists (CES). These individuals assist with on-site bomb investigations, keep field agents apprised of the latest explosive technology, offer technical advice on federal explosives storage regulations, and train federal, state and local law enforcement officers in all aspects of handling and destroying explosive material. The CES agents also respond to incidents where small quantities of explosives are found. A typical call-out, for example, might involve the recovery of stolen bomb material that has not yet been used to build an explosive device. A CES agent would drive out and handle it. This keeps the EEOs doing the render-safe work they were trained for, rather than having to make a lot of trips into the field on non-emergency calls.

CES agents are not allowed to perform render-safe procedures or to work on destructive devices or homemade bombs. They are limited to dealing with raw explosives only. They are trained to handle and destroy up to 60 pounds of explosive material. They have their own equipment, such as a blasting kit and countercharges, to do this. After receiving 5 weeks of initial training, CES agents are recertified every other year.

Beirut. The World Trade Center. Oklahoma City. Nairobi. All of these bombing incidents reinforce the fact that the car bomb is a terrorist's weapon of choice. Recognizing this, the ATF has been researching the effects of large car bombs since 1993. Codenamed "Dipole Might," the project, which has received funding from the Technical Support Working Group and the National Security Agency, is working to design a computer software system to help investigators analyze large-scale car bombings. To accomplish this, the ATF destroys vehicles with as much as 20,000 pounds of explosives—more than four times larger than the bomb that destroyed the Murrah Building.

Working in conjunction with the U.S. Army Corps of Engineers and the Defense Nuclear Agency, the ATF conducts the Dipole Might tests at the White Sands Missile Range in New Mexico. Typically, a car or van is filled with a specific amount of explosive—1,000 pounds of C-4, for example—and is then parked on one of four common road types and remotely detonated. Using a grid system on the ground and GPS measurements, the researchers precisely mark the location of vehicle and bomb fragments, as well as their mass, shapes and sizes. They also gather information on the tremendous pressures produced by the explosion, and residues that are formed by the blast. All of this data is stored on a computer and will help determine an overall blast pattern. This, in turn, can be used by future bomb investigators to predict where they will find evidence at a crime scene. And by comparing the Dipole Might data with the results of a criminal bombing, the investigators can determine the size of the blast, what kind of explosive device was likely used, and how it was constructed.

To date, these tests have been very successful. For instance, they have shown that 15 specific and unique parts of a vehicle *always* survive an explosion. This can be helpful in two ways. First, if one of these parts is found on the street, a bomb tech can measure its distance to the crater. This can hint at the size of the bomb used in the explosion. Second, if a bomb tech is searching for a particular car part for evidence, all he has to do is measure the size of the crater (which suggests how large and powerful the bomb was) and then walk a certain distance to the area where the tests suggest it should be located.

The ATF conducts other bomb-related research at Tyndall Air Force in Florida and at the Federal Law Enforcement Training Center in Glynco, Georgia. Subjects they are looking into include the fragmentation of pipe bombs, explosive residue formation and street sign damage resulting from blast waves. The more ATF bomb investigators know about blast effects, the faster they can solve cases and put terrorists behind bars.

An amazing photograph of what 20,000 pounds of C-4 plastic explosive looks like from 7,000 feet away (with a little help from a powerful camera). The C-4 was stored inside a truck to mimic truck bombs used by terrorists. The ATF conducts such tests to assist investigators in finding evidence that can identify how a bomb was made and who made it. *Bureau of Alcohol, Tobacco & Firearms*

Special Missions

Although pipe bombs are by far the most common explosive device used by criminals today, the ATF must also prepare for more sophisticated devices and unique situations. To this end, the ATF bomb techs have worked with the Department of Energy's Nuclear Emergency Search Team (NEST), reviewing technologies that would be used by NEST and the Army's 52nd Ordnance Group to gain access to a nuclear bomb or an improvised radioactive device. This includes the detection and disarming of booby traps.

One of the unique capabilities of the Explosive Technology Branch is its Underwater Explosives Recovery Team. Five bomb techs, all trained SCUBA divers, have advanced training on how to find and recover explosives underwater. Often the team is searching for evidence to use against a bombing suspect. "What better place (for a criminal) to dispose of explosives or hazardous devices than a pond, lake or river?" asks explosives enforcement officer Johnnie Green.

ATF and the Edmund (Oklahoma) Police Department now cosponsor a week-long school in Evan, Oklahoma, on underwater recovery techniques for other bomb squads. Attendees have to have more than just open water SCUBA training; technical diving skills are required.

This sharing of knowledge is a hallmark of the ATF and its explosives enforcement officers. They routinely train bomb squads and law enforcement officers nationwide in explosives, render-safe procedures, and counterbomb techniques. For the last 10 to 15 years they have also taught postblast investigation courses for Department of State personnel at Site 39, a CIA facility located in Hertford, North Carolina. And, they also train on a regular basis with the Federal Aviation Administration, Environmental Protection Agency, and the Federal Emergency Management Agency.

"There isn't anything I have, or any knowledge in my brain that I won't give to you if your job is to take care of bombs," says Green. "If it will get you home at night to your family, then what I have is yours."

Oklahoma City

On the morning of April 19, 1995, ATF Special Agent Wally Higgins made a quick stop at the credit union inside the Alfred P. Murrah Building before heading to the federal courthouse down the street. Greeted by a long line at the teller window, he decided to come back later in the day. As he entered the courthouse, a Ryder van parked outside the Murrah Building exploded. Higgins ran back and did a quick assessment. Since he had participated in some of the "Dipole Might" test shots (see sidebar "Codename: Dipole Might" for more details on this program), he immediately knew that it was a truck bomb, and called ATF headquarters.

Two National Response Teams were subsequently sent to Oklahoma City, accompanied by five explosives enforcement officers. For Dondi Albritton, chief of the Explosives Technology Branch at the time, it was a horror show. He had been stationed in Oklahoma for 5 years, from 1984 to 1989, so he knew many of the people killed that day. "It was emotional," he says quietly. "I can't describe it. You've got a job to do and you do it, but you're a mess inside."

David Shatzer agrees. "Nothing prepares you for the magnitude of 168 dead people, killed by a man with a personal vendetta. They rewrote the medical books on blast damage to human bodies after Oklahoma City. Children were unidentifiable. . . ."

For the first couple of days, while the main focus was on rescuing survivors trapped beneath the rubble, the ATF bomb techs helped sift through the crater debris searching for evidence. (The debris had been scooped out and

The death and destruction at the Oklahoma City bombing would have been significantly less if Timothy McVeigh had not driven the van so close to the building. By positioning the van as he did, he might as well have driven inside. This photo shows how deep the blast wave penetrated the building. *Mike McGroarty*

hauled to the Sheriff's Department firing range, where it was carefully screened.) They also hunted down key parts from the Ryder truck, relying on data from Dipole Might to suggest fragment trajectories and landing spots. Evidence was eventually recovered up to nine blocks away from the Murrah Building.

What amazed and pleased everyone was the accuracy of the Dipole Might data and how it strongly mirrored what the ATF bomb techs and investigators were seeing at the Oklahoma City bombing. For instance, the vehicle frame had severed where it was expected to sever. The back bumper survived as expected. The rear axle flew off and traveled backward down the street as anticipated. And the residue at the seat of the explosion indeed proved to be from a fertilizer and fuel oil-type bomb.

Once components of the bomb were found in the debris, the bomb techs pulled together to reconstruct the device. By April 29, just 10 days after the explosion, they had built a replica of the homemade bomb. The model was shown to all investigators so they would know what to look for in the way of fragments as they examined the rest of the debris. When the investigation finally came to an end, the model proved to be very much like the real bomb built by Timothy McVeigh, which was painstakingly pieced back together.

One of the things that caused despair and exasperation in every ATF bomb tech was the numerous conspiracy theories that were voiced by right-wing groups that sympathized with McVeigh's motives, if not his actions. They made wild claims (without proof of course) that the bomb was hidden inside the

While rescue workers searched for survivors, investigators from the ATF, FBI and other agencies searched 144 piles of debris for evidence. Using various-sized riddles, it took them a week to go through the piles, which were filled with body parts, money, personal effects, top secret documents, masonry, wire, sheetrock, etc. Each morning, predators, such as coyotes, buzzards, raccoons and possums, that had been feeding on human remains, had to be killed so that evidence could be removed from their throats and stomachs. *Federal Bureau of Investigation*

Murrah Building, not in a Ryder truck parked outside, or that the ATF had explosives stored inside the building and that's what exploded. Other rumors claimed the bombing was a result of a drug buy gone bad, or that the ATF knew about the bomb threat ahead of time and quietly evacuated its agents (and no one else) from the building. For the highly trained ATF bomb techs, stories like these, from ignorant conspiracy-mongers, drove them crazy.

The facts of the matter are these. First, a 4,800-pound bomb could not possibly have been "hidden" inside the Murrah Building. There were too many people working in and around the building to have overlooked someone carting a bomb of that size into the structure. Besides, the blast crater was located outdoors, and not inside the building.

"It's impossible to make a crater appear someplace where it's not supposed to be," says Richard Strobel, a forensic chemist with the ATF Forensic Science Laboratory. "An explosion follows the laws of physics. You can't change it." He also points out that if the bomb had been inside the building, it would have scattered parts of the building itself in an outward direction. This wasn't the case at all. The only thing found scattered outward in a 360-degree manner were parts from the Ryder truck.

Second, the ATF did not store explosives inside the Murrah Building. Third, the bombing was not a result of a drug deal gone bad. The blast was caused by someone angry with the federal government.

And last, the ATF didn't know about the bomb threat ahead of time. If it had, it would have evacuated the entire building.

The ATF managed to reconstruct the bomb used at Oklahoma City within 10 days. The 4,800 pounds of ANFO were stored in plastic containers like this one. The agents were able to build this model based on plastic parts recovered from corpses and the debris field. *Bureau of Alcohol, Tobacco & Firearms*

As it was, two of its own agents were injured in the explosion.

The ATF bomb techs are quick to point out that the damage and death toll at Oklahoma City would have been dramatically less if the truck had not been parked so close to the building. The truck was within 6 feet of the

Sifting through tons of debris for clues is a painstaking and demanding task that only an archaeologist might relish. To accomplish this dirty and distressing duty faster and in a more professional manner, the ATF created the National Response Team (NRT) in 1978. There are four of these teams today, each led by a full-time Team Leader and each responsible for responding to explosive emergencies in a geographic region of the United States. As many as 31 ATF special agents are assigned to each team. Most are special agents with fire and postblast expertise, complemented by forensic chemists, fire protection engineers, accelerant or explosives detection canine teams, and explosives enforcement officers. The team works closely with state and local officials in reconstructing the scene, identifying the seat of the explosion (or origin of the fire), conducting interviews, and sifting through debris for evidence.

Most incidents usually involve only 10 to 12 team members. However, major explosions may require all 30 members, plus others from another NRT. For instance, two complete National Response Teams responded to the World Trade Center bombing and to the Oklahoma City bombing.

There are 35 fully equipped NRT response vehicles scattered across the country. This allows the NRT to respond to an emergency and be on-scene within 24 hours. Each vehicle—which is essentially a self-contained mobile office—is equipped with digging tools, personal protection gear (Tyvek suits for dealing with hazardous materials and firefighter's suits), forensic crime scene surveying equipment, computers for forensic evidence gathering, and state-of-the-art communications equipment. They also carry inflatable tents, which are used to provide additional work space at a scene. When an investigation is completed, all the shovels, picks and other digging tools used at the scene are discarded to prevent carrying explosive residue to the next bombing or arson incident.

Since its creation, the NRT has been deployed 409 times. The teams typically respond to incidents in which property damage is in excess of $1 million or lives have been lost. They also respond to requests for assistance made by local ATF and law enforcement officials. All NRT members work normal duty hours at field offices across the country. They respond to call-outs by going directly to the crime scene after receiving a mobilization order. To prepare for the job they must do, each team member completes a week of advanced training each year in areas such as building collapse, structural integrity, and preserving evidence for legal cases.

A spin-off of the NRT is the International Response Team (IRT). It responds to requests from the State Department's Diplomatic Security Service for assistance in investigating fires and explosions at U.S. properties overseas. The team also provides technical and forensic assistance to foreign governments who request such help through the local U.S. ambassador.

The IRT members are selected from the personnel that staff the NRTs. Since they are not tasked with investigating the crime scene itself, a typical IRT response usually requires only two or three people. Who is sent depends on the nature of the emergency, but generally the team includes an explosives enforcement officer and a forensic chemist.

The IRT has responded to 13 incidents, including two bombings in Peru, which involved large vehicle explosions with improvised devices never before seen, and two bombing attacks made on the Israeli Embassy in Argentina. The IRT also flew to El Salvador to assist the UN Peacekeeping Force, which had recovered a bomb that was meant to kill the UN Secretary General. Similarly, the IRT helped investigate an assassination attempt made against the President of Macedonia. A bomb exploded under the Presidential car, killing the driver and a pedestrian and seriously wounding the President, his security officer, and four bystanders.

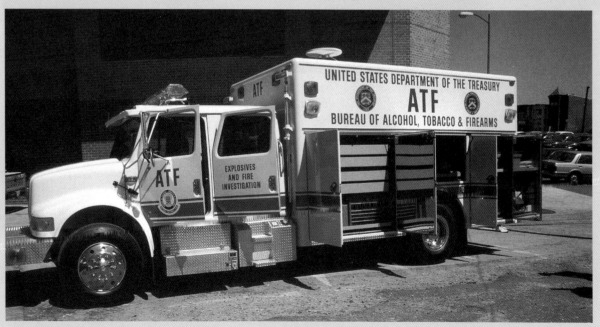

A close-up look at the response vehicle used by the ATF's National Response Teams. There are 35 of these trucks scattered across the nation, all equipped to respond immediately to bombing and arson incidents. *Bureau of Alcohol, Tobacco & Firearms*

An overhead view of the Sandy Springs bombing, which occurred in Atlanta in January 1997. This photo is of the secondary device that exploded; it was targeted at police, firemen and bomb techs who responded to the first bomb. The crater is visible to the right of the telephone pole. Fortunately, cars were parked in the area at the time, and they took the brunt of the explosion. *Federal Bureau of Investigation*

building when it exploded, due to a "cut-out" area in the sidewalk that allowed passengers to be conveniently dropped off by car. If the full sidewalk had been in place, the truck would have been 20-25 feet away. And, as anyone in the bomb disposal field can readily attest, distance is your best friend when it comes to a bomb. By driving to within 6 feet of the building, McVeigh's bomb might as well have been inside.

Strobel agrees. "You essentially had an explosion followed by a building collapse. The architecture of the building was such that if a couple of critical columns go out, this thing comes tumbling down. There doesn't seem to be much of a mystery there."

Preparing for the Future

Car bombings are not the only nightmare for ATF explosives enforcement officers. They know that the world is increasingly becoming a more violent place. Bombers today are much more cunning in their designs than in years past, and they are deliberately making them more deadly. They are adding shrapnel, such as nails, ball bearings, and wire, to achieve larger body counts. Bombers are also targeting first responders with hidden secondary devices, and they are experimenting with chemical and biological agents.

To respond to these threats, the ATF received funding from Congress to upgrade its postblast investigative capabilities. This included the 33 new National Response Team vehicles, which are equipped with state-of-the-art gear and are now deployed nationwide. The ATF also has a new crisis command truck, as well as a portable laboratory, which can be driven straight to a bombing crime scene to provide a variety of on-site lab analyses.

The agency is also in the process of completing N-Force, a case management system that will speed up bombing and arson investigations by creating a computer database capable of searching for commonalties in a given case. N-Force replaces the antiquated Advanced Serial Case Management system (a.k.a. "Ask Me"). It is currently being field tested in Baltimore and should be ready for national distribution by the end of 1999.

In a similar fashion, the ATF is upgrading its National Arson & Explosives Repository. Formerly known as the Explosive Incident System, this is a database that contains technical information on every bomb used in a crime since 1974. It includes detailed listings of bomb parts, how the device was used, unique design features, motives, etc. An investigator can search through all 80,000 investigations to identify a possible suspect, figure out what parts are in a bomb that need to be rendered safe, or determine bombing trends and patterns in any area of the country.

"Any component that's ever been used in a bomb and reported, we have in the system," boasts Stephen Scheid, an explosives specialist who oversees the database.

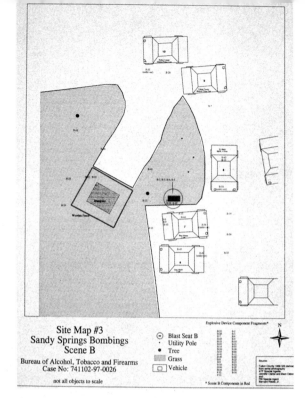

A schematic drawing of the Sandy Springs bombing, as sketched by the ATF. It shows the positions of the cars in the area, as well as the blast seat and recovered fragments. This kind of precise collection of data is what investigators rely on to catch a bomber. *Bureau of Alcohol, Tobacco & Firearms*

A typical query might come from a police officer wanting to know about any car bombings that have occurred during the past 4 years in Chicago involving galvanized steel pipe bombs with clear wiring. Using the repository, he'd have his answer in about 3 minutes. The information he would receive might help him catch a bomber before he or she strikes again.

Although the ATF has passed the lead to the FBI and U.S. Marine Corps with regard to chem-bio incidents, the agency is still prepared to respond to such an incident. They know that their expertise in explosives and in postblast investigations are always going to be needed. It is a reality that no one denies.

Chapter 5

The Montgomery County Bomb Squad

It was a hot and hazy summer afternoon in 1997, and U.S. Supreme Court Justice Sandra Day O'Connor had just been dropped off at her Montgomery County, Maryland, home by her security detail. As she walked up the steps, she noticed an unmarked box wrapped in black plastic sitting next to the front door. Her security officers, immediately suspecting the worse, whisked O'Connor away to safety and called the Montgomery County Fire & Rescue Services to check out the package. Since Montgomery County did not have a bomb squad at the time, it called upon the State Fire Marshal's office to send a unit.

As everyone waited for the bomb squad to arrive, police set up a perimeter and evacuated all the homes in the immediate area. Then the FBI arrived, followed by the news media, which began broadcasting live reports about the "bomb scare."

O'Connor was watching the news coverage on a TV at a nearby country club when a friend casually said something like, "Gee, doesn't XYZ shoe company wrap and mail their shoes that way?" With a sinking feeling in the pit of her stomach, Justice O'Connor realized that she had indeed ordered some shoes from that company recently.

At around this same time, a United Parcel Service driver, who had delivered the package, heard about the incident on his radio. He called the police and was immediately patched

> ## *We take a lickin' if it stops tickin'*
>
> – Popular Bomb Squad T-Shirt

through to the command post set up at O'Connor's home. The driver informed officials on the scene that the package contained a pair of tennis shoes. When he had delivered the box, he had inadvertently placed it face down, which is why the box appeared to be unmarked. The address and return labels were hidden from sight.

By this time, the bomb squad had arrived. After learning about the UPS driver's call, a bomb technician was sent down to examine the box. When he opened it up, he found the tennis shoes. They were safe and sound.

New Kids on the Block

Although this humorous incident brings a smile to most faces, it demonstrates what a potentially dangerous world this can be. Terrorists, who are ever willing to resort to violence to achieve their goals, typically keep an eye out for a target who can gain the public's attention through his or her gruesome death. Hence, politicians, diplomats, corporate CEOs and celebrities are all fair game for the determined bomber. Understanding this tenet, one of the most target-rich areas in the United States is Montgomery County, Maryland. This densely populated 605-square-mile tract of land, located on the outskirts of Washington, D.C., is where many important diplomats, corporate executives and top-ranking government officials live. It is also home to well-known corporations like IBM,

Captain Sam Hsu of the Montgomery County bomb squad approaches a suspect chemical-type bomb. He doesn't know if it contains an incendiary liquid like gasoline or a chemical warfare agent like Sarin. This uncertainty is growing today with terrorist-bombers resorting to more sophisticated and deadly devices. *SF Tomajczyk*

Lockheed Martin and Marriott, and to federal agencies like the Nuclear Regulatory Commission and the National Institutes of Health. All are tempting targets.

District Chief Brian S. Geraci, assistant fire marshal, knows this fact all too well. "This is a very target enriched county," he says grimly. "There is a lot of potential for acts of terrorism."

This reality played a major factor in Geraci's efforts to create a county-based bomb squad that could respond not only to explosive devices, but to chemical and biological threats as well. The problem was that there was no money available. So the fire and rescue department made special arrangements with the county government to do public fundraising. By the end of 1997, just months after the O'Connor incident, enough money had been raised and in-kind services donated, that the department was able to establish a six-member bomb squad.

Although it is one of the newest squads in the nation—it became operational in January 1998—the team has managed to acquire nearly everything it needs to provide sophisticated counterbomb services to the county and the state. For instance, it has a Med-Eng search suit, a manipulator arm, two Royal Arms disrupters, and a handheld Golden X-ray system. Additionally, the military donated six bomb suits; the ATF provided a Safeco bomb suit and a single-vent containment vessel; the FBI supplied a PAN disrupter; the NRC donated another X ray system; and a local body shop converted a donated ambulance into a modern bomb truck, all for free.

"A lot of people recognized the need for our bomb squad," says Geraci. "They understood that terrorism is here in the United States, and that a fast-response capability saves lives. They wanted a local bomb squad that could get to a device quickly and take care of it. So they supported us. In fact, many

A ballistic shield gets a quick check-over before being stored aboard the bomb squad truck. Such shields offer bomb techs a bit more protection when they have to remain on-target longer than they'd like. *SF Tomajczyk*

people were shocked to learn that that Montgomery County didn't have its own bomb squad before now."

The bomb squad is now focusing its efforts at getting a larger bomb truck, a Remotec Mark 6 robot, an EOD-7B bomb suit from Med-Eng Systems, and a real-time X-ray system. The latter piece of equipment, which is computer driven, allows the bomb technicians to digitally enhance X-ray images of a bomb's components so they can clearly see what they are dealing with. If it ends up being something unusual—a strange initiator of some sort—they can send the image by modem to agents at the FBI's Bomb Data Center for advice on how to "attack" it safely. All of this can be done within just a few minutes.

The six members of the bomb squad are all fire investigators, with a rank of lieutenant or higher and at least 3 years experience in that role. All of them have successfully gone through the FBI's Hazardous Devices School.

The team commander is Captain Sam Hsu. Geraci has scheduled their staff so there is a minimum of one bomb tech on every shift, plus Hsu or himself. When a bomb threat is called in or if a suspicious package is found, the unit responds with three people, who assume the following roles: Operations Officer, Entry Tech and Safety Tech. Their responsibilities are fairly straightforward. The Operations Officer oversees the entire response, the Entry Tech does the actual render-safe procedure, and the Safety Tech watches out for the safety and well-being of the Entry Tech while on-site and offers back up assistance when needed.

During an average month, the bomb squad responds to about 10 bomb threats. In 1996, there were 125 call-outs; in 1997 there were 90. Most of these incidents involved military ordnance, improvised explosive devices and hoaxes.

"It's busier than I thought it would be," says Geraci.

The inside of a well-organized and well-equipped bomb squad truck. Bomb suits are stored in canvas bags on the floor to facilitate easy access. The shelves hold hand tools, rigging equipment, evidence containers and diagnostic gear. *SF Tomajczyk*

69

Taking careful aim at a bomb hidden inside a box, which was confirmed by an X-ray. The bomb tech aims the barrel of the disrupter at the bomb's power source, hoping to knock it out and prevent the bomb from detonating. *SF Tomajczyk*

Terror in the Schools

One of the surprises for the Montgomery County bomb squad is how many incidents occur in the county's school system. In the first few months of 1998, for instance, the team responded to four bomb threats, including one involving a binary chemical, gas-expansion device in a middle school. Fortunately, the teenager had not mixed the chemicals when the bomb squad showed up.

This was a disturbing incident, but it wasn't nearly as alarming as a case that happened at the Rocky Hill Middle School in Clarksburg, Maryland, during February 1998. A 13-year-old boy we'll call "Joe" became upset at the funeral of his grandmother, when his distraught mother accused her father of sexually molesting her when she was a child. Joe overheard the accusation, and decided to seek revenge by killing his grandfather. He asked a friend of his, whom we'll call "Larry," if he knew of anyone who could build a bomb. Larry said that he did know a high school student we'll call "Michael," who knew something about explosives. Joe had Larry ask Michael to build a bomb for him, and he did.

The device that Michael built was essentially a can of ether strapped to several CO_2 cartridges filled with powder taken from a model-rocket engine. An explosive incendiary bomb, it could be electrically fired using a 100-foot-long length of wire and a battery. Michael designed the bomb so that it easily fit inside a backpack. All Joe had to do was place the bomb where he wanted it, run out the length of wire, attach it to the battery, and BOOM! His grandfather would be dead.

Joe decided to have a friend drive him out to his grandfather's house that upcoming weekend. He intended to place the bomb inside his grandfather's car and then patiently wait for him.

Fortunately, when Larry, the middle man, brought the finished device to school that Friday to hand it over to Joe, kids on the school bus saw the bomb. "We love kids, because they love to talk," smiles Assistant Fire Marshal Geraci. "They love to show things. They can't keep a secret."

And in this situation, they certainly didn't keep the bomb's existence to themselves. After arriving at school, some of the students went to the principal and told him about the homemade device. Since the principal had had a disciplinary encounter with Joe several weeks earlier, and since a rumor was going around that Joe was going to blow up the principal's car, the principal decided that he'd take a look inside Joe's locker to see if there was indeed a bomb.

Sure enough, when he opened the locker, he saw the backpack. Taking a quick peek inside, all he noticed was the can of ether and a bunch of wires. He didn't see the CO_2 cartridge, but that was enough for him. The police and bomb squad were called, the school was evacuated, and Joe was brought to the principal's office.

When Geraci and the bomb squad arrived, they knew there was a live bomb. What concerned them though, was the possibility of a secondary device being hidden somewhere. They asked an explosives canine team from the Montgomery County Police to conduct a search for them. To better protect the dog handler, who was only wearing a Kevlar jacket and helmet, they loaned him their ballistic Med-Eng SRS-5 search suit. He and his dog then systematically checked the lockers, hallways and the principal's car for explosive devices. They found nothing.

While the search was being conducted, one of the bomb techs interviewed Joe. At this time, no one realized that the real target of the backpack bomb was not the school principal, but Joe's grandfather. He didn't admit that until later. In fact, he didn't even admit that the bomb in his locker was his. In spite of this, he did provide a sketch of what the device looked like at the technician's request.

"He drew us a lovely picture of the device, so we knew what we had," says Geraci. "He didn't admit to having it, but he drew us a nice picture anyway."

Two bomb techs were sent in to disarm the homemade bomb—one to do the actual procedure and the other to serve as a backup. First, they set up rigging and carefully removed the backpack from the locker. Then they took an X-ray of it to figure out where the power source was positioned. Once they had a good idea of where to aim their PAN disrupter, they fired. The water charge ripped the bomb out of the backpack, but failed to disrupt it. It was still intact. So they shot it again, this time using a Clayvon round. Although the CO_2 cartridge was torn away from the can of ether as the bomb techs intended, the can detonated. The explosion left a scorch mark on the floor and started a small fire, which was quickly extinguished by the bomb techs.

Over the weekend, fire investigators collected evidence, interviewed witnesses and suspects, and searched the students' homes. All three boys were arrested and temporarily placed in a juvenile facility. When Michael was interviewed, he told the investigators that he had learned how to build bombs from another high school student. So the investigators went to that teen's home and collected materials. Although he was not involved in this incident, he had played the role of mentor. He was charged and then released to the custody of his parents.

As for Michael and Larry, they both entered guilty pleas and were subsequently placed on home detention. They were also suspended from school. Thirteen-year-old Joe was eventually charged with attempted murder after police learned why he had ordered the bomb built. He pleaded guilty and received a four-month sentence in a juvenile detention center.

What amazed bomb technicians and investigators about this incident was the age of the defendant and the seriousness of his intentions. Assistant Fire Marshal Geraci points out that although children are naturally attracted to fireworks and bombs, it takes a certain type of child to decide to actually build a bomb. He says that most young bombers are between the ages of 12 and 18, with an interest in the Internet and chemistry. They are very intelligent and they "hang" with small groups of friends, numbering no more than five. Many of these children are also dealing with peer pressure and socialization issues.

"You wouldn't believe the stress some of these kids have," he says. "They bare their souls to us, how much pressure they're under."

A picture of the future: bomb techs and hazardous materials technicians approaching an apparent chemical-type device (lower left). Assistant Fire Marshal Brian Geraci is having his bomb squad and HazMat team train together so they are prepared for the real thing. It is only a matter of time before terrorists resort to chemical or biological agents here in the United States. *SF Tomajczyk*

Preparing for the Nightmare

While youths may indeed be under a lot of stress today, it doesn't compare with the concern that the Montgomery County Fire & Rescue Service personnel have about the inevitability of dealing with a chemical or biological terrorist attack some day. It may be a binary chemical bomb hidden inside a corporate headquarters, or it might be the release of anthrax spores over the city. It could even be an underground attack on the Metro subway system using a poison gas like Sarin, which was used in the Tokyo gas attack. In all of these instances, it will be the county's bomb squad and the HazMat team responding to it, which is why they are training so hard now.

Geraci, who has 16 years of experience dealing with hazardous materials, firmly believes in integrating the two units together. "A chem-bio incident is essentially a modified HazMat incident. Instead of dealing with a spilled cleaning liquid like sodium hydroxide, we're dealing with a bomb or dispersing device that can spew chem-bio agents all over."

He also notes that bomb techs and HazMat personnel take the same approach when dealing with emergencies like these and are familiar with the proper procedures and equipment. For instance, they both evacuate the danger area; identify hot, warm and cold safety zones; deny entry; use diagnostic tools and sensors; and wear protective gear.

"With HazMat and bomb disposal, it's a slow process," he says. "We're not quick to rush in, like firefighters attacking a fire. We gather facts, do a hazard risk assessment, and then figure out a plan and our options."

Hence, the 40 men and women on the county's HazMat team have been trained to support the bomb squad. They've learned how to assist the bomb techs in putting on and taking off their bomb suits, and how to use some of their equipment. When a possible chem-bio incident arises, both HazMat units respond. Their huge, specially equipped vehicles are outfitted with chemical and biological detection gear, including draeger tubes and reactive chemical agent strips. Additionally, the vehicles carry several Tyvek F suits, which responders can quickly don to protect themselves from exposure to chemical warfare agents like Sarin and VX.

Once they arrive on site, a reconnaissance team consisting of one bomb tech and one HazMat operator carefully examines the device. Each team member looks at the device from a different perspective, which is good. "The HazMat guys bring a lot of experience and tools to the game," stresses Geraci. "They may see something that the bomb tech may not immediately notice, and vice versa."

This concept of merging bomb disposal and HazMat together is novel, but more and more emergency-response teams around the nation are following suit. Geraci notes that he recently met someone from Riverside, California, whose unit is doing this, but it was originally initiated by callouts to clandestine drug labs. Now they're doing it for possible response to a chem-bio threat.

What keeps Geraci awake at night is not preparing for a chem-bio attack but convincing every man and woman in the department to take the threat seriously. To make sure they do, all 1,600 firefighters in the Montgomery County department have received training in chemical and biological terrorism, know what signs and symptoms to be alert for, and how to work in a contaminated site. The department feels that proactive education is a good way to overcome firefighters' fears of being involved in a chem-bio incident.

"I think we're prepared. I think we have the resources in place to deal with an incident," says Geraci. "We don't want them to be afraid. "We want them to be able to go in and do their job, and make viable rescues.

POOF! Dressed in special protective clothing, a HazMat technician tests the air for the presence of a chemical warfare agent like Tabun or VX. The red box lying on the ground (center, rear) is a special Chemical Agent Monitor. It will sound an alarm if a deadly gas is present. *SF Tomajczyk*

But, obviously, we don't want them to become victims either. If they keep their wits, take precautions and limit their time, everything should be okay."

To ensure this, the department has conducted research to determine how chemical agents penetrate a firefighter's suit and what he can do to thwart this from happening. Testing was done at the Aberdeen Proving Ground, home of the Army's Chemical & Biological Defense Command.

Secondary Threats

Chemical and biological terrorism aside, there is another danger confronting emergency personnel—secondary devices. These are bombs deliberately hidden and aimed to harm the firemen, EMTs, HazMat operators and bomb technicians who respond to an initial bombing. It is a very real threat, as demonstrated by bombings in Alabama and Georgia.

The single most important factor that prevents injuries and deaths from occurring in situations like this is distance. The further away a first responder stays from the crisis scene, the less likely he is to be struck by shrapnel from a secondary device when it explodes. That's because the bomber assumes that the responders *must* go into the blood and gore to assist people injured in the first incident. Hence, he has positioned the secondary device so that it is aimed at ground zero.

Assistant Fire Marshal Geraci says that his department teaches emergency responders that they have to avoid rushing in until a search is done for secondary devices. As cold and callused as it may sound, the bodies of bomb blast victims who are obviously deceased should be left in place to allow for the collection of debris that may have forensic value. Injured patients should not be treated at the scene except in unusual circumstances. Instead, they should be quickly moved as far as possible from ground zero to a secure area for treatment and triage.

This recovery effort should be accomplished by as few responders as possible. Only when the scene is determined to be safe and free of secondary devices should a full rescue and investigative effort be launched.

Geraci also warns his bomb techs of being "sucked in" to a scene by the police or the person who found the bomb. All too often, he says, bomb techs arrive to find a police officer waving them toward the device, which is usually near his feet. Instead, the bomb techs should tell the officer to come to them (without the device in hand, obviously).

"Distance is a bomb tech's best friend," he says. "Cops don't necessarily know this. So retreat and expand the perimeter."

Geraci has also witnessed situations in which police officers have opened packages to see if there was a bomb inside and, he related one case where an officer actually used a stethoscope to listen to a package. "He informed us when we arrived that the package wasn't ticking, so he went ahead and opened it up. Our jaws hit the floor in amazement."

Actions like this are not rare; it's a universal problem with police nationwide. Even police bomb squads have a difficult time teaching their peers not to open a package just because it "looks safe."

Fortunately, training efforts are under way across the United States to better educate police officers about how to properly handle potential bomb situations. The Montgomery County bomb squad has joined this effort and now offers a training course that drills the message home by hiding a few fake bombs in the classroom desks. When an officer opens a drawer, he is greeted with a blinding flash and a loud buzz. The lesson? "Don't be curious. Don't open stuff up."

Future Endeavors

Since Montgomery County sits adjacent to Washington, D.C., the seat of freedom and democracy, its bomb squad and HazMat units

Assistant Fire Marshal Brian Geraci stands in front of his county's hazardous incident response vehicles, which are equipped with state-of-the-art equipment. Being so close to Washington, D.C., and having politicians living in Montgomery County, Geraci knows that he has to be prepared to respond to the most sophisticated attacks. *SF Tomajczyk*

will likely have to respond to a large bombing incident in the capital someday. To ensure that its units are able to respond quickly to such crises, Geraci is working with the FBI and the U.S. Marshals Service to deputize the members of each team. That will give bomb squad and HazMat staffers the legal authority to cross state borders in an emergency. At this time, only the department's arson dog team, consisting of fire investigator Lieutenant Wayne Shaw and his Labrador retriever, Tipper, is deputized. This permits them to assist with arson investigations all along the East

Coast. They also serve with ATF's National Response Team

Planning for the future like this is natural for Geraci. He knows what terrible things can go wrong, and he wants to make sure that his teams are prepared for the worst scenarios. Thus, he constantly strives to obtain the necessary funds to buy new equipment. And he also ensures that his bomb squad and HazMat teams stay on top of their training.

"You can never get complacent," he says. "The face of terrorism is constantly changing. We can't let our guard down."

Chapter 6

U.S. Capitol Police: Hazardous Devices Section

Unlike other federal buildings, which have secure perimeters and restricted public access, the U.S. Capitol is one of the most open and accessible structures in America. That's because citizens expect to be able to visit with their elected representatives without hindrance. As a result, visitors freely roam the hallways of the building and pedestrians and cars constantly come and go at all hours of the day.

"It's always a bomb until you can prove it's not."

Detective Dave Novak, U.S. Capitol Police, HDS

"In all the years, I've never seen two (bomb calls) exactly alike. Something's different on each one."

Sergeant Ray Eaton, U.S. Capitol Police, HDS

If, however, a lunatic or terrorist wants to make a statement through violence, the Capitol is the ideal location, with all 535 members of Congress being potential targets for bombings and assassination. In fact, several people have already tried to attack the Capitol with bombs during this century.

In July 1915, for instance, the Senate reception room was damaged by the explosion of a homemade bomb built and placed there by former Harvard University professor Erich Muenter. He was upset by the private sales of U.S. munitions to the Allies in World War I.

In March 1971, a bomb exploded in a first floor bathroom of the Senate Wing. Two explosive devices were supposedly used in this incident, both hidden in place over the span of two days. The second device triggered the other bomb's detonation, causing extensive damage but no injuries. The incident, which was allegedly done by the Weather Underground, came at a time of rising opposition to U.S. policies in Vietnam.

In 1980, a man using a pickup truck loaded with an incendiary bomb, attempted to smash through the south wall of the Capitol after first leading police on an erratic chase through the city. He was eventually caught and arrested on the lawn outside the Capitol before any serious damage resulted.

In October 1983, an Israeli entered the House Gallery with an improvised explosive device that contained some 4.5-pounds of homemade black powder. He demanded world peace and threatened to detonate the bomb, which was wired to a hidden switch. Fortunately, the device was not built correctly and it failed to detonate. After his arrest, the police discovered that he also possessed detailed diagrams of the Capitol chambers.

On the evening of November 7, 1983, a bomb planted by an extremist group known as the Armed Resistance Movement exploded

Since the U.S. Capitol is the ultimate symbol of democracy in the world, the U.S. Capitol Police has one of the best-trained and best-equipped bomb squads to protect government leaders from terrorist bombings. Immediately following the July 1998 shooting at the Capitol, which resulted in the deaths of two brave officers, the bomb squad was sent in to make sure the shooter had not also planted a bomb. The subsequent search didn't find any hidden devices. *SF Tomajczyk*

A look at ground zero of the 1983 bombing that took place inside the U.S. Capitol on the second floor, just outside the Senate Chamber. Fortunately, no one was hurt in this incident, but it did spur Congress to fund more projects to beef up security. The bomb was hidden behind the cushions of an alcove seat. *U.S. Capitol Police*

on the second floor of the Capitol, in an alcove just outside the Senate Chamber. The explosion damaged a conference room and the offices of Senator Robert Byrd of West Virginia. The bomb contained five pounds of dynamite stashed inside a gym bag and was hidden behind the cushions of a hallway bench. Fortunately, the Senate had retired earlier than expected that evening—the Washington Redskins were playing on Monday Night Football—and no one was nearby when the bomb exploded just after 11 P.M. An anonymous caller phoned *The Washington Post*, claiming that the action was in response to U.S. military aggression in Grenada and Lebanon.

And in 1984, a Molotov cocktail was thrown by a disgruntled person and it ignited on the Capitol Rotunda steps, injuring a bystander.

At the Heart of the Action

Although horrifying, each of these acts spurred Congress, and thus, the U.S. Capitol Police, to enhance security measures. As a direct result of the 1971 bombing, Congress approved the installation of a closed-circuit television system so that police could monitor the activities of visitors to the Capitol. They also approved the formation of two special units for the Capitol Police force—an explosives detection canine section and a bomb squad.

The Hazardous Devices Section (HDS) was created in 1974 with six bomb technicians. Captain Gilman G. Udell, Jr., oversees the unit in his role as commander of the department's Technical Security Division. He is the last active duty member of the original team. The others have since either transferred to other positions or retired from the department.

Unlike the Montgomery County Bomb Squad, which is a new unit with limited, but growing, experience and assets, the Capitol Police HDS is an established and highly capable team with access to prototype, state-of-the-art equipment that other bomb squads around the nation are not even aware of. This is primarily because of the importance of its role in protecting the seat of America's government. As you can imagine, the technology gives them a distinct edge over the bombers.

The HDS is now composed of 10 bomb technicians, all of whom have successfully completed training at the FBI's Hazardous Devices School and advanced counterbomb training elsewhere. In fact, many of the bomb techs have undergone chemical and biological warfare training at the Army's Chemical Center &

Because of the city environment and the fragile nature of the ancient buildings, the bomb squad has a total containment vessel (TCV) to suppress bomb blasts and capture fragmentation. It is carried on a powerful and specially made bomb truck. The unit also has a remote-control Andros Mark V-A robot, which is shown here placing a pipe bomb inside the TCV. *SF Tomajczyk*

The Hazardous Devices Section is one of the few bomb squads in America to have been trained in chemical and biological warfare. Their bomb techs have attended the Army's chemical school in Alabama. The squad's response vehicles are all equipped to handle chemical attacks, including atropine kits to keep exposed victims (and themselves, if necessary) alive. *SF Tomajczyk*

School at Fort McClellan in Alabama. The school features a state-of-the-art training and simulation center known as the "BIDS Bunker." BIDS stands for Biological Integrated Detection System.

The chemical-biological threat was clearly illustrated in April 1997, when police cordoned off a two-block area around the B'nai B'rith building in Washington, D.C., and quarantined 108 people after a suspicious leaking package was found in the mailroom. The package contained a red liquid in a Petri dish marked "anthrachs"—a misspelling of the disease anthrax. The dish was also emitting a foul odor, but thankfully turned out to be a hoax. Although the incident was handled by the Metropolitan Police and the FBI, it got the full attention of the Capitol Police HDS. They realize that it is only a matter of time before a valid attack occurs, and the Capitol is a high profile target.

On any given day, some 18,000 visitors wander the 40 blocks surrounding the Capitol building, which encompasses the small but important jurisdiction of the U.S. Capitol Police Department. This number can swell to crowds of 100,000 people or more during protests and special events, such as the Independence Day celebrations. A dynamic and changing environment such as this challenges the bomb techs, who find themselves constantly responding to abandoned briefcases and suspicious, double-parked cars. Technically, anything that is delivered to Capitol Hill has to be inspected by bomb techs or explosives detection canines. Over the years, the HDS has examined a variety of strange objects, including boats, and even a pile of coal, which was dumped on Capitol Hill by protesters.

The bomb techs are also responsible for sweeping the U.S. Capitol building itself every day, looking for any hint of hidden explosives. In a methodical fashion, they examine the critical areas of the building and the surrounding lawns before Congress arrives for work in the morning. They even search the elevator shafts. In one incident at the Rayburn House Building, people riding in an elevator heard what they thought was a ticking clock. Fearing the worst, they ran out and called the bomb squad. After evacuating the area, one of the techs climbed on top of the elevator and found a piece of paper jammed in the ventilation fan.

Additionally, HDS searches buildings and public areas ahead of the arrival of high-level government officials, including the President of the United States, foreign dignitaries and heads of state. They work closely with the U.S. Secret Service on these assignments.

The most demanding and time-intensive events for the bomb team are those involving the Presidential Inauguration and the annual State of the Union Address. On these occasions, the U.S. Capitol Police bomb techs are responsible for sweeping the venues for explosive devices and maintaining constant security. This is particularly difficult when you consider that security must be maintained 24-hours a day while the scaffolding is being built for the inauguration, weeks before the event itself. All materials being used in the framework, booths and displays must be carefully examined before they are allowed to be brought on-site and used. Bombs with time-delay or remote-control triggers can be hidden inside wooden beams, pipe railing, and concrete.

Although most of the bomb squad's work is done during the day, the unit provides counter-bomb coverage during the evening and late night hours as well. All bomb technicians are on call 24 hours a day to respond to emergencies.

The Selection Process

Positions with the Hazardous Devices Section are few and far between, since it has a maximum of 10 bomb technicians at any one time. Yet, retirements, transfers, and promotions do occur, opening up a slot from time to

It's amazing what a little water can do to a bomb. This close-up shot captures a PAN disrupter using water to rip a metal box containing sticks of dynamite apart. Water charges are the most commonly used shot by bomb techs. *SF Tomajczyk*

time. In these instances, the HDS refers to a list of candidates who have successfully passed an initial screening process. This consists of meeting minimum physical requirements and department standards, going before an oral review board, and passing a practical exercise. The latter is important, since it indicates whether or not a candidate has the suitable skills and temperament for bomb disposal work.

Essentially, the practical exercise has the candidate wearing a bomb suit—to see if he is claustrophobic—and walking 300 yards or so with X-ray equipment and a disrupter to a fake bomb. He then sets up the equipment, and returns to his starting point. The candidate also must complete various drills while wearing the bomb suit to demonstrate his agility and physical fitness.

Senior members of the HDS look for candidates who are open-minded and who want to learn new things. "We don't want somebody coming to this unit who's a 'know-it-all,'" says Captain Gil Udell.

Once a candidate passes this initial selection process, he is ranked in comparison to other applicants and placed on a candidate list. When a position opens up, the top candidate on the list is sent to the FBI's Hazardous Devices School for formal training. Once the FBI course is complete, the new bomb tech spends a year on probation with HDS, going out on calls and assisting with counterbomb efforts.

The training is never ending. Bomb techs get plenty of on-the-job learning by responding to suspicious packages, they also attend advanced and specialized courses offered by federal agencies and the military. Additionally, the unit experiments with new equipment and practices new render-safe procedures on explosive devices at nearby Quantico Marine Corps Base in Virginia. The Marines have been long supporters of the U.S. Capitol Police and the HDS.

Since all the bomb techs have received the same training and have worked so long together, they often seem to read each other's minds. For example, when they respond to a bomb threat, the men instinctively and efficiently go about getting the necessary gear out of the bomb truck and setting it up.

"We all know what the other guy's thinking," smiles Udell. "That's what we want in a new bomb tech. We want someone who'll work with us, not against us."

As with most other bomb squads around the nation, the HDS bases its response around a two-man team concept. One bomb tech works on the package while the other assists. Once deployed on a bomb threat, the individual ranks of the technicians go right out the window. Everyone becomes an equal—there are no sergeants, captains or lieutenants. Every bomb tech's opinion matters and is heeded. This prevents a technician from getting married to one idea on how to handle the situation; it may be the wrong idea.

Bombs hidden inside car trunks can be exposed with a carefully aimed disrupter shot. Here, a bomb tech is in the beginning stages of setting up a PAN disrupter. He will likely use a water charge or a low-velocity slug to safely open the car trunk. *SF Tomajczyk*

"It's a group effort," says Detective Dave Novak, a bomb technician. "You're partners. The rank dies as soon as you go on a package."

Toys for the Big Boys

Because it is tasked with protecting Congress, HDS has resources and equipment that are the envy of other departments. The bomb techs use the Andros Mark V robot to do surveillance and remote render-safe work. The robot rides around in the bomb squad's specially built truck, which has a Total Containment Vessel on the back. The TCV is ideal for use in a congested city environment, since it traps both the debris and the blast wave from an exploding device. (The unit has no single- or double-vented containers.) This eliminates any damage that could be done to Washington's numerous architectural wonders, many of which date back to the late 1700s and early 1800s.

In addition to the bomb truck, HDS also has two other vehicles, a Chevy Suburban and a pickup truck. The pickup is typically used to haul explosives for countercharge use and training purposes, since it is equipped with a government-approved box that allows both the blasting caps and explosives to be carried together. A metal wall separates the two.

The unit also owns a station wagon emergency-response vehicle, which carries all of the necessary equipment to respond to a bomb threat, such as a PAN disrupter and ammo, Med-Eng EOD-7B bomb suit, X-ray gear and film, and a chem-bio suit. The latter item is an interesting one. The Capitol Police HDS was one of the first bomb squads in the nation trained to deal with chemical and biological terrorist attacks. Up until now, its technicians have used the military's Level C protective gear, but they are now upgrading to a more sophisticated outfit that features a self-contained breathing unit, and not just an air filter.

In light of the chem-bio threat, the HDS uses a laser aiming device on its disrupters so that it can target specific components inside a package or bomb. In the past, bomb techs have used the disrupter to make a general shot at the bomb container, knowing that it would likely scatter the components and thereby prevent an explosion. However, with a chem-bio device, this approach cannot be used. The last thing you want to do is haphazardly break open a vial containing a potential chemical agent or biohazard. That's where precision disrupter shots are needed.

Sergeant Ray Eaton, an HDS bomb tech and the former president of the International Association of Bomb Technicians & Investigators, agrees. "The decision that the bomb tech makes out there means a lot as far as breaking something apart and spreading it around."

In the event that the bomb techs have to operate in a chem-bio environment, the unit has special chemical solutions at its disposal for decontaminating personnel and equipment. Atropine kits are also included in their gear to act as an antidote in case a bomb tech comes into contact with a deadly nerve gas like Sarin, Tabun or VX.

HDS members sit on a variety of research & development committees, including the Technical Support Working Group, a federal interagency committee established in 1986 to develop technologies and prototype equipment that can be used in the fight against terrorism. This includes gear for bomb disposal work. Because of this affiliation, the HDS has direct input into what technologies it needs to defeat the bomb-making advancements of terrorists. Many of the resulting prototype items have been field-tested by the HDS, such as a mineral water bottle disrupter developed by Sandia National Laboratory many years ago. Following in this manner, the HDS is likely to be an early recipient of future state-of-the-art counterbomb technologies.

Captain Udell is quick to point out, however, that possessing technology doesn't automatically solve all your problems. "No matter how many great toys your department has," he says, "They're no good if you can't practice. You've got to train, train, train."

For instance, an X-ray is no good if a bomb tech cannot interpret the image. The same holds true for other counterbomb equipment. A disrupter is no good if a bomb tech doesn't know what kind of load to use. If he goes too heavy, he could detonate the device. If too light, it won't do anything. Udell says bomb techs have to constantly familiarize themselves with their equipment.

"It's become more of an art *and* a science."

What the %$#@ Is It?

Every bomb squad has a favorite bomb story to tell, and the U.S. Capitol Police is no different. One of their more memorable and challenging experiences occurred in the early afternoon on January 3, 1995. A suspicious item was reported at Third and Independence Avenue. With the Republican Party about to take control of Congress, the HDS took the threat seriously, feeling that perhaps a disgruntled person was trying to send a deadly message to the politicians.

When the bomb techs arrived on scene, they set up a perimeter and approached the device to take a quick look. What they found was a very large pipe bomb—the largest one, in fact, that they had ever seen. It measured about 2 feet long and had a diameter of about 6 inches. From outward appearances, it was obviously made by a professional bomber. Everything was perfectly fitted.

They took an X-ray of the bomb, which revealed a fine gauge wire running through the device and a filler of some sort. So they set up their PAN disrupter and took a shot. Then another. Both efforts failed.

The bomb techs exchanged glances of amazement and wondered what the hell this thing was. The bomb's outer casing was so hard that the disrupter didn't even dent it.

Sensing that they had a very unusual bomb on their hands, they decided to transport it away from the Capitol area. "We wanted to get it out of the city and into a safe area where we could work on it," recalls Sergeant Eaton.

The HDS team used its Andros Mark V robot to move the device into the total containment vessel, which was on the bomb truck. Then they drove to Poplar Point and patiently waited for the evening rush hour traffic to subside. Three hours later, after darkness fell, they drove to Quantico Marine Corps Base in Virginia . . . with a little escort help from the Virginia State Police.

"We went right up Route 95 with a full motorcade flashing red lights," says bomb tech Lieutenant Mike Conway. "It looked like a Christmas tree."

When they arrived at one of Quantico's ranges, they were greeted by representatives from the FBI and ATF, as well as generators powering huge outdoor lights. After the pipe bomb was removed from the containment vessel by a robot, the bomb techs decided to use a linear-shaped charge to breach the casing. The Marines donated one of their explosive charges, and it was successful in cracking the bomb open. The bomb techs were greeted with the sight of a tube filled with white sand and some wiring.

What was it? Well, it turned out to be an electrical fuse. A 13,000-volt fuse, to be exact. The same kind you might find in your basement electrical box, albeit much larger and used in Washington's Metro subway system. It seems this fuse fell from a truck and rolled to a stop at Third and Independence, where it was eventually found and thought to be a pipe bomb. Ironically, the fuses are normally packaged in pairs. Had the second fuse fallen

Is it a pipe bomb? Well, if it looks like one, smells like one and sounds like one, it must be one. That's what the bomb techs thought, too. As to what it really was, the surprise answer is hidden in the text. Read on. *SF Tomajczyk*

off the truck as well, the bomb techs would have found writing on it clearly identifying it as an electrical fuse. That would have ended the "bomb incident" hours earlier and avoided all the flashing lights and pandemonium.

The HDS bomb techs still get a chuckle over this event. They later sent the 13,000-volt fuse to the FBI's Hazardous Devices School so that it could be used as a teaching tool for other bomb technicians.

Deadly Serious

Although the previous incident made a lot of people laugh, it didn't become lighthearted until the very end, when the bomb techs finally learned what they were dealing with. Because of their job and because of where their job is located, the bomb techs of the U.S. Capitol Police are quite serious about what it is they do. Every team member knows that the next phone call could be the deadly threat that they have all dreaded.

If the phone does ring, it won't be the first time. In 1976, the Chilean ambassador was killed by a car bomb in Washington, D.C. He was driving through the city (not too far from the U.S. Capitol) with his secretary and her husband, when terrorists used a pager to detonate 2.5 pounds of explosive hidden under his seat. When the bomb exploded, it blew off the ambassador's legs, killing him instantly, and sent a piece of metal slashing into the throat of the secretary, who was sitting in the passenger seat. Her jugular vein severed, she literally drowned in her own blood within a few minutes. The only survivor of this atrocity was the secretary's husband, who was seated in the rear of the car.

The members of the U.S. Capitol Police bomb squad understand that an event like this will happen again. It's inevitable, given the deadly terrorists that exist in our often chaotic world. But they stand ever vigilant to respond to a call and prevent death and disaster from happening. They go to preserve our government and the American way of life, and to protect the ultimate symbol of freedom in the world, the U.S. Capitol.

The dog is man's best friend, and has been for thousands of years. Over the centuries, people have used dogs for herding, tracking, hunting, and assisting the disabled. In the past 50 years, dogs have been introduced to the law enforcement arena. Their dedication, intelligence, and keen sense of smell make them ideally suited for the fight against terrorism.

> *"Dogs are still one of the best tools. We have yet to find an explosive odor that the dogs don't hit on."*
>
> –Robert Noll, Explosives Enforcement Officer, ATF

Dogs are routinely used today by numerous federal agencies, such as the U.S. Customs Service, U.S. Park Police, and Secret Service. They are used to provide physical security, detect drugs and contraband, and also in counter-bomb efforts. Additionally, many state and local law enforcement agencies, and all branches of the armed forces, use canine teams.

Pros and Cons

It should be noted that there are some disadvantages to using dogs as explosives detectors. Cost is one concern. It's expensive to buy a dog, train it (and its handler), and provide on-going veterinary and kennel services to keep the dog healthy and productive. Additionally, a vehicle must often be purchased and maintained to transport the canine team. Because of this, agencies with tight budgets find it difficult to justify the establishment and operation of a canine explosive-detection team.

Second, dogs do not operate by themselves. They always work in tandem with their handler, who is responsible for recognizing the subtle changes in the dog's behavior that indicate the presence of an explosive. Reliance on this judgment introduces opportunities for mistakes. For instance, if the handler is bored and not alert, the team is likely to miss targets, even if the dog is performing well.

When compared with electronic sensors, dogs have other weaknesses. Unlike machines, they are vulnerable to distraction by other animals, loud noises, novel scents, fatigue, illness, airborne pollutants, and new surroundings. Additionally, dogs cannot work for extended periods of time. Depending on the weather conditions, a dog may only be able to work 20-30 minutes before requiring a rest.

And last, dogs can respond to the wrong thing. For example, dogs have been known to respond to such things as shoe polish, VCR tapes, nitroglycerin pills, and electrical tape. These items contain elements that are typically found in explosives. Furthermore, since dogs rely on smelling airborne molecules, they may not be able to detect an explosive if it is tightly wrapped or sealed.

So why use dogs at all if these drawbacks exist? Quite simply because they are

The U.S. Capitol Police Department's 30 canine teams conduct some 23,000 searches every year for bombs and explosives on Capitol Hill. They search cars, people, and the Capitol itself. It's an important job, saving the lives of political leaders and foreign dignitaries, and ensuring the continuity of our government. *SF Tomajczyk*

The Connecticut State Police has long been involved in training dogs for law enforcement use. Connecticut officers worked with the ATF in 1986 to train Mattie to detect accelerants, and in 1992 they assisted in training the ATF's explosives dogs. This picture shows a Connecticut State Police dog searching through the debris at the Murrah Building in Oklahoma City. Dogs like this were brought in to locate secondary devices and unconsumed explosives. *Federal Bureau of Investigation*

very effective. There is no mechanical sensor on the market today that is as fast, accurate, sensitive, mobile or durable as a well-trained dog team. And since they operate right on the scene, they can signal the presence of an explosive far quicker than a machine, pinpointing a bomb's location.

Thus, while canine teams are expensive, they are cost-effective. Their appearance alone often hinders bombers from carrying out their deadly deeds.

Selection and Training

Among mammals, rats and dogs are credited with having the best sense of smell. In fact, most dogs are able to detect a vapor at concentrations up to 10,000 times lower than humans. Pigs also have an excellent sense of smell, but their use by police has been ruled out for obvious reasons.

Although many breeds of dog are suitable for explosives detection, most law enforcement agencies prefer German Shepherds, since they can be cross-trained for patrol work, which requires aggressive behavior. The Secret Service uses German Shepherds and a breed called Belgian Malanois. The Malanois is a breed developed in Europe during the early 20th century by crossing Shepherds with hounds.

The ATF, however, is dedicated to using Labrador Retrievers, which are less expensive, more mild mannered and longer lived than a German Shepherd. They are also said to have better noses.

Regardless of the breed that is chosen, any dog being considered for explosives work must be in excellent shape and relatively young, ideally 12 to 18 months, and no more than 24 to 36 months. In general, only males are used (especially if they are to be cross-trained for street patrol) because they are larger and more aggressive than female dogs. Many agencies acquire their dogs through public donations.

Once a dog is selected, it is matched up with a handler, and both of them go through several months of training. During this time, the dog is taught obedience work, both on and off the leash, how to respond to verbal commands, and how to cope with a variety of obstacles.

As for explosives training, the dogs are typically taught a three-step sequence: smell the explosive compound, alert, receive a reward. Depending on the agency's training philosophy, the reward can be food, praise or play. After doing this 70 to 150 times, the dog comes to realize what is expected of him. The process is repeated for each explosive that the dog is expected to detect. Most dogs are trained to find about 15 of the most common military and commercial explosives, such as TNT, C-4 and Semtex.

In some agencies, the dogs are taught how to follow a scent cone to the location of the strongest odor. Scent cones are the downwind waffings that emanate from a bomb. The dog learns to weave back and forth through this cone, moving upwind toward its source. To assist with this process, the handler is trained to observe environmental conditions and interpret the dog's behavior. He works the dog in a search pattern that takes advantage of air currents.

When a dog picks up the scent of an explosive, he physically responds to it by salivating, bracketing or quickening his pace. The handler learns to recognize when the dog is exhibiting this behavior. The Secret Service teaches its canines to signal the presence of an explosive by alerting and then sitting down. The last thing they want the dog to do is bite or shake a suspicious package.

Overall, federal agencies use more than 3,000 dogs, with the military employing some 1,600. The military prefers working with German Shepherds, since their more-aggressive demeanor ideally suits them for guard duty, in addition to explosives detection work. *U.S. Army*

Once the dog and handler have completed the course, they are ready for field work, but formal training does not end at this point. During work hours, the handlers challenge the dogs by hiding training aids scented with different explosive compounds. This is done at varying locations and at different times of the day. The concentration of the explosive is also randomly altered.

The dog returns to its agency's training facility on a regular basis for refresher courses and recertification. During this time, he is tested against several explosives that he has not recently encountered. This ensures that the dog is still properly responding to the whole range of explosive threats.

Searching for Bombs

The handler has the last word when it comes to determining the readiness of his dog for an assignment. This is because the handler and dog usually live together. Hence, the

Running like the wind, a dog rushes up a hill to retrieve a "Kong," a rubber toy that the U.S. Capitol Police use to test a dog's suitability for explosives detection. The trainers tend to look for dogs that are intelligent, inquisitive, brave and energetic. *SF Tomajczyk*

handler knows his animal inside and out. He can tell if the dog is being distracted, or if he is ill or fatigued. If the handler doesn't feel the dog is performing properly, he or she has the right and obligation to remove the animal from service without fear of being overruled by a supervisor.

The ability of a dog to detect an explosive depends on several things, including the terrain, the temperature, the humidity, and the amount of air movement. On hot, humid summer days, for example, a dog can detect explosives much easier than on a cool, crisp day. That's because in warm conditions, more explosive molecules are evaporated, saturating the air. The major drawback of hot days, obviously, is that the dog can only work 20 to 30 minutes before requiring a break. Also, if the dog is searching a paved area, the blacktop can become very hot, burning the dog's feet and

nose. Heat exhaustion is a concern, which is why handlers keep water on hand for the dogs to drink and cooling vests for them to wear.

A typical car search begins with the canine team approaching the vehicle downwind. This gives the dog the best chance of detecting odors. Some handlers, like those with the Secret Service, carry a small smoke generator to help them determine wind direction and speed, thereby characterizing the size and shape of the scent cone.

The dog is given a command to search the vehicle. Together, the dog and handler circle the car in a counterclockwise fashion. The handler has the dog pay close attention to the locks and any ventilation outlets. This is because some cars are so tightly sealed when the doors and windows are shut that it can be difficult for odors to escape. Because of this, the driver is often asked to open the trunk.

A vehicle search takes about 30 seconds to accomplish. If, during the search, the dog is interested in an area but does not alert, the handler notes the location, finishes the search and brings the dog back for a recheck. If the dog alerts at any time during the search, he is immediately rewarded and the bomb squad is called in to investigate. Handlers do not handle explosives or do render-safe procedures. Their sole task is to detect the presence and location of explosives.

As for room searches, the canine team is always brought in *after* the room has been canvassed for booby traps. The bomb technician's search procedure divides the room vertically by height –floor to waist, waist to chin, and chin to ceiling. The technicians overlap search areas for better coverage. Only when the room is found to be free of booby traps is the dog team allowed to begin its search.

It should be noted that dogs are not 100 percent accurate in their detection efforts, and

The ATF uses only Labrador Retrievers for explosives detection, since they have great sense of smell. To date, the ATF has trained more than 160 dogs, which are now in 10 countries. Here, a Retriever searches for the scent of an explosive hidden inside a sterile container. One or more of the containers may have an explosive compound . . . or a distracting scent, like food. To pass, the dog must ignore everything but the explosive. *SF Tomajczyk*

should not be expected to provide that level of accuracy. In fact, most law enforcement agencies consider a dog to be efficient if it is able to correctly detect an explosive 90 to 95 percent of the time while in training. This translates into a "street-wise" proficiency of about 75 to 80 percent. Dogs are *never* punished for giving a false alert. In the realm of explosive devices, false positives are tolerable, whereas false negatives are not.

Military Explosive Detector Dogs

Since the Civil War, trained dogs have been used by the U.S. military forces for guard and patrol duties. The training of military dogs is conducted at Lackland Air Force Base in San Antonio, Texas. The majority of the dogs are purchased in Germany and northern Europe from selected breeders. German Shepherds are usually used, and are between 12 and 36 months old when they begin their training. Shepherds are at least 23 inches high at the shoulder, weigh 60 pounds or more, are in excellent shape, and have a mildly aggressive disposition.

The dog's basic training course is broken into nine distinct phases. Early on, the handler learns the principles and techniques of reward, and how to give verbal and manual obedience commands. As the training progresses, the dog learns how to work at greater physical distances from the handler and how to respond to gunfire. The dog is also taught to master various obstacles that it will encounter during actual situations, such as tunnels, windows and elevated catwalks.

The later training phases address more advanced topics such as patrolling methods, building searches, intruder detection, vehicle patrolling, and tracking.

Upon completion of the course, the dog is certified and then either sent to a military installation or used at Lackland Air Force Base for training other handlers. The dogs are generally not trained as explosives detectors until the need for such an animal arises. When it does, the dog/handler teams undergo additional training, with the dogs achieving a 95 percent accuracy rate in detecting explosive items. The dogs are trained to detect a variety of explosives, including ammonium nitrate dynamite, nitroglycerin dynamite, C-4, TNT, water gel, det-cord and smokeless powder. Navy dogs are also trained on black powder, in the form of a time fuse. In addition, military dogs are trained to detect two types of pharmaceuticals, potassium chlorate and sodium chlorate, that are often used in explosive compounds, and firearms that have been previously fired.

Explosive detection dogs undergo recertification every 3 months. The validation test are made up of trials involving at least five of every substance for which the dog is trained, and never less than 20 in total.

When it comes to searching for an explosive device, the team searches in a counterclockwise fashion, keeping as low as possible. The search is ended before the suspect item is touched or picked up by the dog. This is because many explosives are poisonous, and the bombs in which they are used are sometimes equipped with movement-detection devices.

Unlike most law enforcement agencies, military explosives detection dog teams are always accompanied by a spotter while conducting the search. A spotter is a person who is trained with the team and, hence, is as familiar with the dog's behavior as the handler. He works ahead of the team, looking for booby traps and other hazards, and the spotter also

Uh oh! Charlie's found something. See how still he is? See that gleam in his eye? See his handler reaching for food to reward him? That's right, he found the container with the explosive compound. Good dog! *SF Tomajczyk*

describes to EOD technicians the area in which the dog alerts to an explosive. Lastly, the spotter monitors a clock to ensure that the dog team is not on target too long and can be safely evacuated prior to a known detonation time.

U.S. Secret Service

The Secret Service, which protects the President and other dignitaries, has one of the largest nonmilitary canine bomb detection units in America. Established in 1975, its 35 Canine Explosives Detection Teams search structures, vehicles and individuals for various threats, including bombs. The Secret Service gets its dogs, German Shepherds and Belgian Malanois, from a breeder in the Netherlands.

Training, which lasts 20 to 26 weeks, is done at the Secret Service's Canine Training Facility in Beltsville, Maryland. Small groups of new dogs and rookie handlers, typically four or five, are trained about every two years as retirements deplete the unit. The Secret Service uses four dog trainers who are civilian employees of the agency. However, the dog handlers are selected from the ranks of uniformed Secret Service agents. They are chosen based on their seniority and an evaluation of how well they work with the dogs. The only physical requirement is the ability to carry 80 pounds, which is the average weight of a dog.

At Beltsville, the dogs learn how to deal with obstacles and how to chase down a suspect. They are also taught to find 13 types of explosives. They do not train on peroxides, which are too unstable to work with. The dogs are taught to sit when they find a potential explosive.

Every dog returns to the Beltsville facility each week for a full day of continuing training as part of a recertification process. The dog is tested against three or four explosives other than those used by his handler during the previous week. If the dog fails, he returns to Beltsville for additional training until he proves that he can respond to the entire range of explosive threats.

A typical day for a canine team might include working at the White House for several hours sniffing a motorcade, and then spending the rest of the day patrolling the grounds of embassies. The dogs go everywhere Secret Service protectees go. This sometimes involves overseas travel. In these instances, they travel like other animals, in cages in the plane's baggage compartment. Not all dogs enjoy this, however. Like people, they can be fearful of unexpected turbulence, and they can suffer from jet lag. Dogs have been known to wash out of the program due to an inability to cope with travel.

It is important to note that dogs are not the sole means used by the Secret Service to find explosives. They are just one tool of an overall bomb detection effort.

U.S. Capitol Police

With the number of government officials working on Capitol Hill and the frequency of visiting dignitaries, it is not surprising that the U.S. Capitol is heavily guarded against terrorist attacks. In 1971, the U.S. Capitol Police established its first canine team in response to a bombing incident in the Senate wing of the Capitol. The canine unit consisted of 12 dog teams, all trained for street patrol. Six of these dogs were later trained in explosive detection.

Since then, the Canine Unit has expanded to a total of 30 dog teams, all of which are capable of detecting 14 different types of explosives. Each team has undergone 26 weeks of intensive training at the Unit's headquarters, which is located at the former Metropolitan Police Department's K-9 training facility in Blue Plains. The training includes on- and

Nope, it's not the "Wheel of Fortune." But there is a prize hidden inside one or more of these cans, and it's *not* a trip to Bermuda. The trainer spins the wheel and the dog has to find the container that holds the explosive compound. It's important to note that not all training is so controlled: the ATF routinely takes the dogs out into the field to be exposed to different environments, like airports, warehouses, and courtrooms. *Bureau of Alcohol, Tobacco & Firearms*

off-leash obedience commands, obstacle navigation, evidence searching, tracking, building searches, criminal apprehension, and handler protection.

Nearly half the 12-week course is dedicated to explosives detection. This training is completed before the 14-week-long street patrol training, because the department places a priority on a dog's ability to detect explosive compounds. If the animal is unable to detect explosives, he is removed from the program. (Explosives work is so important that the department intends to expand the training from 12 weeks to 16 weeks.) In order to pass, the dogs must attain 100 percent accuracy in identifying explosive odors and 80 percent overall proficiency. The dogs return every month for 16 hours of remedial training.

Additionally, every Canine Explosive Search Team is required to conduct a practice search each month, using explosives provided by the department.

The Canine Unit works exclusively with male German Shepherds. They once considered using Belgian Malanois, but found them to be too aggressive to deal with the Capitol building's 18,000 daily visitors.

This may change in the future. The department is looking at the possibility of bringing on Labrador Retrievers to do explosives work, exclusively. The dogs have a reputation for having a great nose for explosives.

Presently, the department's German Shepherds are acquired from public donations, animal shelters and breeders. Most of the dogs range in age from 12 to 30 months old, with 24 months being the preferred age for training. They serve for 5 to 7 years before being retired. All dogs live with their handlers at home.

To determine whether or not a dog is a good candidate for explosive search work, the instructors test the dog using a black, conical-shaped toy called a "Kong." Several trials are conducted. For example, an instructor may step on the Kong and see how the dog responds. If he tries to dig and dislodge it, it demonstrates that the dog is inquisitive and intelligent, which is a good sign. In another test, an instructor suddenly opens an umbrella or clangs two trash can lids together while the dog is playing with the Kong. If the dog cocks its head out of curiosity and holds his ground, instead of startling and running away, it shows that he has courage. Again, another good sign.

All the training is done at the Canine Unit's headquarters, which features five acres of classrooms and open fields, an obstacle course, indoor and outdoor kennels, and storage facilities.

The selection of dog handlers is based on their past police performance, experience on the street, physical condition, plus his or her attitude toward and basic knowledge of dogs. The evaluation also may include interviews with the applicant's family and neighbors.

The Canine Unit teaches its handlers to use both play and food as the dog's reward. Because of this, you'll find a Kong in every canine scout car. The search teams are used to sweep the grounds of the U.S. Capitol every day, as well as to conduct advance counter-bomb work for dignitaries traveling in and out of the Washington, D.C. area.

The dogs are also assigned to monitor permanent posts such as the delivery area for packages coming into the Capitol and any ongoing protection assignments. They also search vehicles parked along the streets adjacent to the Capitol and support arrests made by the Police officers in the area. The U.S. Capitol Police canine vehicles (a.k.a. scouts) are designed to transport two dog teams. All tolled, the dog teams conduct some 23,000 explosive searches each year.

Whenever explosives are found, the department's Hazardous Device Section is immediately notified. The canine teams are not authorized to disarm bombs. That task is left for the bomb techs.

Alcohol, Tobacco and Firearms

As America's lead agency when it comes to explosives and postblast investigations, the Bureau of Alcohol, Tobacco and Firearms has been involved with explosives-detection techniques for decades. In a 1984 pilot program, the ATF trained the first dog to detect accelerants, which are chemicals used by arsonists to make a fire burn faster and more furiously. Detecting these chemicals is essential in establishing whether arson caused a fire, and finding the person responsible. The dog, a Labrador Retriever named Nellie, helped establish the feasibility of this new detection system. In May 1986, the first operational dog, Mattie, began training in conjunction with the Connecticut State Police and hit the field in September of that year. Since then, the ATF has trained and certified 56 accelerant detection dogs, 47 of which are working with fire departments, police departments, and fire marshals' offices across the country. The ATF's National Response Teams and field offices also have access to these dogs when needed.

Based on the success of this program, and the fact that the ATF investigates the majority of all bombings in America, the agency used the knowledge gained from the accelerant program to create the Explosives Detection Canine Program in 1992. This program was formed at the request of the State Department, which needed dogs to send to foreign countries in support of its antiterrorism efforts and to protect American travelers. Since 1992, a total of 160 dogs have been trained and certified for use in 10 different countries, including Italy, Israel and Australia. All of these dogs are able to detect minute quantities of explosives, and can find firearms and ammunition hidden in luggage, in vehicles, and on people, as well as buried underground.

Much of the initial canine training was done at facilities owned by the Connecticut State Police. But this changed in 1995 when the ATF entered into an agreement to share the facilities at the U.S. Customs Canine Enforcement Training Center, a 250-acre complex located in the Blue Ridge Mountains near Front Royal, Virginia. The ATF is now constructing its own administration building, which will house classrooms and a training area large enough to accommodate three simultaneous training classes, on the site.

Although various breeds of canines are used in law enforcement, the only breed used by the ATF for explosives detection is the Labrador Retriever. That's because the Retriever is not only hardy, intelligent, adaptable and nonaggressive, but it tends to use and rely more on its nose than any other breed. "They conduct their lives with their nose," says Robert Noll, an ATF explosives enforcement officer. Retrievers also get along with strangers, which is important because ATF dogs often interact with crowds, as they did at the 1996 Olympics. The dogs are acquired from Guide Dog Foundations, which raises them in family environments until they are about 14 months old.

The ATF's explosives training program is unlike those used by other agencies. After examining several training programs, the ATF realized that there was no consensus on what explosives should be used to train the dogs. Most programs focused on a variety of commonly used explosives, like TNT and nitroglycerin dynamite, but they overlooked improvised explosives. However, recent incidents like the World Trade Center bombing and the Oklahoma City attack have used improvised explosives, such as urea nitrate and ammonium nitrate fuel oil.

Recognizing that it is impossible to train a dog to detect all 19,000 known explosive compounds, the ATF managed to classify these explosives into five distinct families. From this, it identified 20 explosive odors that would best train its dogs to respond to a variety of bomb materials. By using pure samples of the major explosive compounds in each chemical family, the ATF is able to have its dogs recognize nearly any type of explosive.

As for the training method, it is based on a food reward system. Every time the dog "alerts" correctly to the presence of an explosive, he is fed. This system allows the dogs to be subjected to many training repetitions in the course of a work day by measuring out small portions of food. This can't be done with other reward systems, such as play or praise.

During a typical training day, a dog smells an explosive odor 125 times. The dog is *never* fed without exposure to an explosive odor. (Even during a routine work day, the handler tests the dog with numerous explosive odors to feed the dog until he eats his daily ration.) This conditioning stimulus means that the dog can train and work for longer periods, and can work with any handler who feeds him. The latter is a distinct advantage over the widely used "bonded team" concept, which is used by other agencies. ATF dogs can still work when their normal handler is ill or unavailable.

Dogs train with their handlers for 10 weeks. During this time, the dogs are exposed to explosive amounts varying from 1 gram to more than 1,000 pounds. In one training scenario, 3 grams of an explosive is placed in a sterile container, which is perforated with small holes. The container serves to focus the dog's attention on the object and will prevent accidental ingestion. It also hides

In Montgomery County, Maryland, the explosive detection canines are handled by the police. Here, a canine searches some suspicious-looking barrels for the presence of explosive compounds. The police department hopes to add two new canines to its unit. *SF Tomajczyk*

the color and shape that distinguishes some compounds, thereby preventing the dog from using visual cues. The dog is rewarded with food when he alerts properly.

Moving up the scale in difficulty is the "Training Wheel," a device consisting of four containers on a rotating wheel. One container holds the explosive while the others contain either nothing or samples with distracting odors. The dog, searching on- and off-leash, has to discern which container holds the explosive. By spinning the wheel, the trainer can easily present the dog with a new challenge. Furthermore, the explosive compound can be changed at any time, and more than one container on the wheel can hold different explosives or distracting samples. A dog is considered well-trained when he ignores a food distracter in favor of the explosive odor.

At the end of training, the ATF certifies its dogs on 20 different explosive compounds in quantities ranging from 1.7 grams to 15 grams. Two of the odors used are from samples of explosives that were *never* taught in training. This proves that if the dogs are trained using ATF's five families of explosives, they will be able to detect *any* explosive mixture made from them. "We have yet to find an explosive that these dogs can't find," says Noll proudly.

To be certified, a dog must pass this test with 100 percent accuracy on all 20 compounds. If the dog misses an explosive or makes more than two false alerts, he fails. The ATF is the only program with proficiency standards this high. The dogs are recertified annually, with the same strict standards.

The ATF's explosives-detection program has been very successful. Over the years, its dogs have been credited with finding a bomb, which had been missed by human teams searching a bus. They have also found munitions buried in the desert, guns hidden in sacks of flour, and a pistol stashed away in the glove box of a locked vehicle. The dogs also found an explosive device hidden in a purse during a sweep of a courtroom.

This partial list of accomplishments more than justifies using trained dogs in America's counterbomb efforts.

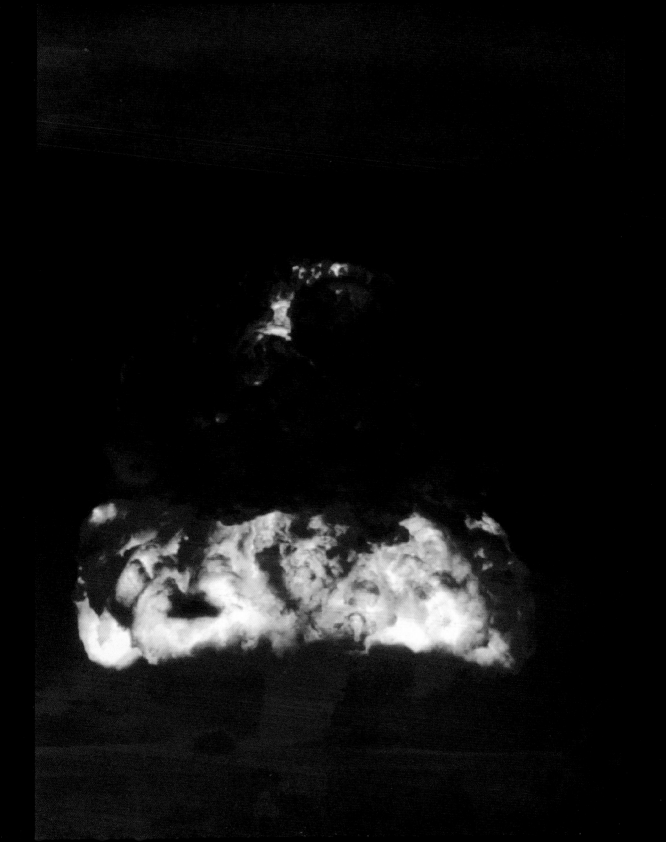

Chapter 8

Weapons of Mass Destruction

It was a simple-looking box, but deceptively deadly. To the bomb technicians who arrived at Harvey's Wagon Resort Casino in Stateline, Nevada, on August 28, 1980, the 2,000-pound metal box sitting on the second floor of the casino resembled a washing machine . . . and an ugly one at that. Besides the steel plates making up the box, the only thing that could be seen were 28 toggle switches, which were neatly aligned in rows on the top. From outward appearances, it didn't seem very dangerous. Yet, hidden inside was a bomb tech's worst nightmare—seven independent firing circuits attached to explosives. At the time, it was the most sophisticated improvised bomb that had ever been encountered in the United States.

The bomb had been pushed into the casino by the bomber and an accomplice, both disguised as workmen wearing overalls, in the wee hours of the morning. The device, which rolled along on caster wheels, was covered by a plastic tarp marked "IBM." Using an elevator, the two men rolled it up to the second floor and armed it. They left behind a three-page extortion note, which was discovered by security officers.

> **"We now know that terrorists are willing and able to use large explosive devices, and devices that disburse chemical agents without warning."**
>
> –Victor H. Reis, U.S. Department of Energy

After evacuating the casino and setting up a safety perimeter, the FBI and local law enforcement officials conferred with Army EOD technicians and the Department of Energy's Nuclear Emergency Search Team (NEST) to figure out how to disarm the device. A NEST robot and X-ray source from the Lawrence Livermore National Laboratory re-vealed that the bomb was not a nuclear device but, it was filled with about 830 pounds of unigel dynamite.

The bomber was demanding $3 million dollars. In return for the money, he promised to disclose the correct sequence of how to flip the toggle switches to disarm the bomb. There were two problems with this approach. First, the bomber said that he would *mail* the directions to the FBI after receiving his money. This was not acceptable, especially given the possibility that the directions might never be sent. And second, FBI agents felt they couldn't trust the extortionist to tell the truth. Not surprisingly, none of the bomb techs wanted to be the guinea pig sent in to flip the switches.

And so the authorities tried to figure out how to disarm the "washing machine." They quickly realized that the bomb maker was as

A scene no one in America wants to see or experience: the fireball of a nuclear weapon. Yet, this threat still exists, even with the collapse of the Soviet Union. Radioactive materials can be bought on the black market and information on how to construct a crude-but-functional nuclear bomb is readily available. This photo is of a 1954 15 MT bomb test conducted at the Bikini Atoll. Its codename was "Operation Castle/Bravo Event." *Lawrence Livermore National Laboratory*

99

In 1980, this weird-looking device found at Harvey's Wagon Resort Casino happened to be the most sophisticated homemade bomb that the United States had ever encountered. It featured numerous antitamper devices, which prevented bomb techs from disarming it. Today, a model of this bomb is located at FBI headquarters to serve as a reminder to bomb techs that they need to be ever vigilant for the unusual. *NAVSCOLEOD*

clever as he was evil. He had installed numerous booby traps to ensure that the device would explode regardless of what the bomb techs attempted. For example, the bomb contained a pendulum to act as an antimovement device and a toilet floater arm as an antifloating device, and the bomb was lined with foil to prevent any penetration. Thus the bomb technicians couldn't move it, flood it with water to short the circuits, or cut through the welded plates. In fact, they couldn't touch the bomb without fear of detonating it.

After 33 hours of analyzing the bomb, authorities finally decided to use a linear, shaped charge to sever the smaller, top box from the larger, bottom box, thereby disrupting the bomb's firing mechanism. It was their only option, since they had no other tools to penetrate the 3/8-inch thick steel plates. The Army provided the necessary explosives to build the cutting charge. It was carefully put in place by the Tahoe-Douglas Bomb Squad and then detonated. Unfortunately, the molten jet of the shaped charge did not form as expected and the bomb exploded, destroying the lower floors of the casino.

Although the extortionist was eventually arrested and prosecuted, this incident marked a turning point in the world of bomb disposal. It marked the arrival of sophisticated improvised explosive devices and spurred bomb squads to develop the necessary equipment and procedures to respond to future incidents of this nature.

This message was reinforced 13 years later, in September 1993, when a device eerily similar to the Harvey's Casino bomb appeared at the Sparks Nugget Casino in Sparks, Nevada. This time, the steel-box "bomb" was chained to a pillar in the casino's restaurant. Compared with the Harvey's Casino bomb, this device was less sophisticated in design, with sloppy wiring and a telephone keypad. This haphazard approach was matched by the extortionist's demands—only $100,000 instead of millions of dollars. All of this made the FBI suspicious and had many believing the device to be a hoax.

Unlike the Harvey's incident though, NEST conducted a *full* deployment this time, sending in hundreds of technicians and lots of high-tech equipment. NEST's analysis of the bomb by diagnostic sensors revealed that it was not nuclear. In fact, the steel container was mostly

When bomb techs attempted to sever the top box from the lower box with a shaped linear charge known as a "Poofer," the bomb exploded. The entire lower portion of the casino was destroyed, as seen here in this amazing photograph. *NAVSCOLEOD*

empty, except for some kitty litter on the bottom. There was no detonator, no initiator and no power source. In other words, no bomb. So the container was removed from the casino, taken to a cook-off point and then opened up.

This case has never been solved, and the FBI has never heard from the extortionist since his one and only phone call in 1993. But for a few nervous hours on that autumn day, the incident reminded bomb techs across the country that huge, homemade bombs were possible . . . even nuclear ones.

The Nuclear Dilemma

Nuclear bombs pose a very real threat to the United States, and not only those that tip the nuclear missiles deployed by hostile nations. Homemade bombs built here in America by antigovernment groups and bombs

smuggled into the country by terrorists are both very real threats. In the past, two things prevented lunatics from building such devices—the knowledge to build the bomb and access to radioactive material. Today, there are no hindrances. Information on how to build a crude-but-effective nuclear bomb has been widely available since the late 1970s, and a black market now exists through which radioactive material can be purchased for the right amount of cash.

To make a nuclear device, all a terrorist needs is to get his hands on 18 pounds of plutonium 239 (an amount about the size of a grapefruit) or 55 pounds of highly enriched uranium. If he can't manage that, then he has the option of finding some radioactive waste, packing it around a few sticks of dynamite, and then setting it off in a populated area.

NEST uses the MD-500 "Little Bird" to detect nuclear bombs hidden in a city. The helicopter is outfitted with sensitive gamma and neutron detection equipment, which is complemented by search teams on the ground. Aerial surveillance aircraft are housed at the Remote Sensing Lab at Nellis Air Force Base in Nevada and at Andrews Air Force Base in Maryland. *NAVSCOLEOD*

When it explodes, the radioactive contamination and subsequent deaths would be horrific.

The collapse of the Soviet Union has contributed to the threat posed by nuclear bomb makers. With that nation's demise, security at its nuclear facilities has waned tremendously. In 1993, for instance, two nuclear fuel rods—each 10 feet long—were stolen from a fuel assembly area at the Chernobyl nuclear power plant and disappeared. This happened in spite of the fact that the reactor building was supposed to have high security. In 1995, 13 pounds of uranium fuel from a Soviet naval reactor was seized by authorities in Kiev.

These are just two of the many incidents that have been reported in recent years, and Russia is not alone. In 1994, 130 barrels of enriched uranium waste disappeared from a storage facility in South Africa. This demonstrates that theft can occur wherever nuclear materials are found. In 1994, more than 687 pounds of nuclear material was confiscated by authorities from traffickers around the world—and that's only what they managed to catch. Plutonium fuel elements (which can be hand-held since they are not highly radioactive) come in hockey puck-shaped disks that weigh a few tenths of a pound. They are easy to conceal in a pocket.

America's Nuclear Ninjas

Nuclear terrorism arrived on United States soil in 1974, when an extortionist threatened to blow up Boston with a nuclear bomb if he didn't receive $200,000. To prove that his threat was credible, he sent officials schematic drawings of the bomb. Their seeming authenticity gave everyone heart palpitations. At the time, the United States had no way to respond to such a threat. Arrangements were quickly made to pay the ransom, but the extortionist never picked it up. Was the bomb a hoax, or did it truly exist? And if it was real, where is it today?

This incident caused the government to create the Nuclear Emergency Search Team in 1975. Known as "Nuclear Ninjas," this unit is operated by the Department of Energy's Office of Emergency Response. NEST is tasked with finding and disarming nuclear bombs, as well as providing technical support to the FBI, which has jurisdiction in cases involving domestic nuclear threats. The team is composed of more than 750 volunteer scientists, engineers and technicians from the national laboratories and other agencies. Key components of NEST are located at Nellis Air Force Base in Nevada and at Andrews Air Force Base just outside Washington, D.C. The team works under the authority of the FBI for domestic crises and the State Department for foreign incidents.

Since NEST was created, the team has evaluated more than 110 threats and mobilized itself to respond to about 30 of them. The team's first deployment took place only a few months after it was established. In November 1975, an extortion letter was received by

Union Oil in Los Angeles. The letter itself was made from words cut and pasted from newspapers and magazines:

> Dear Mr. Hartley:
> There's a nuclear device with a
> potential of 20 kilotons concealed
> on one of your valuable properties,
> electronically controlled in Los
> Angeles County. You will not call the
> authorities . . . Place one million
> dollars, small bills . . .
> *Fision*

Fortunately, this incident, as with all the others since then, was a hoax. But that could change with the next phone call . . .

When the FBI receives a nuclear bomb threat, it passes all information to Threat Assessment Teams at the Department of Energy. These teams, which are scattered around the country, are made up of scientists, weapons experts, linguists and psychologists. At least three of these teams review the data and independently determine if the threat is valid and whether or not a critical mass can be achieved by the bomb. They also decide whether the terrorist has the resolve to actually detonate the bomb. In the end, the answer they give must be a definite yes or no. "Maybes" are not allowed.

As part of this assessment process, the FBI and DoE run the terrorist's letter and any other information they have through a special computer at the Lawrence Livermore National Laboratory. This computer compares the data with published documents about nuclear weapons, including newspaper articles, scientific reports, and even Tom Clancy techno-thriller novels. If the terrorist lifted a phrase from a novel and used it in the extortion letter, the computer will quickly know it. This suggests to the FBI

A laboratory on wheels, ready to be placed aboard a plane and flown anywhere in the world. NEST has five cargo pods: photo lab, generator, video lab, communications lab, and a mechanical lab. This photo is of the photo lab, which comfortably seats one technician and provides that person with all the equipment needed to develop and enlarge aerial photographs and radiation-sensitive films. *Department of Energy/NOO*

that the terrorist may not know what he is doing, since he is plagiarizing.

If the FBI determines that the nuclear threat is credible, it asks the Department of Energy to deploy NEST, which then assembles its high-tech search and detection equipment. Much of this material is already prepackaged for fast deployment. In fact, entire miniature laboratories can be wheeled aboard an aircraft when the Air Force flies NEST to the crisis site. The team can be en route within 4 to 24 hours, depending on the emergency and the type of equipment that is needed. Likewise, the size of the team varies with the nature of the threat.

The Hunt for Nuclear Bombs

The first crucial task in a nuclear crisis is to find the bomb. This is not as easy as it sounds, especially considering that a briefcase-sized bomb is possible and would really be like finding the proverbial needle in a haystack—especially when it comes to searching in a city the size of Chicago or Los Angeles. To achieve this, NEST divides the target city into a search grid and uses aircraft, helicopters and vans to search the area with

Two NEST searchers check out a stadium during an exercise, likely Mirage Gold, which was done in October 1994 in New Orleans. The briefcases they carry are actually gamma ray detectors that sense the presence of a nuclear bomb. When radiation is detected, an alarm is sounded in small earphones worn by the searchers. The detection equipment can also be carried inside innocent-looking backpacks and coolers so as not to alarm the public. *Department of Energy/NOO*

gamma ray and neutron sensors. These sensitive devices detect changes in natural radiation that may suggest the location of the hidden nuclear bomb.

Supporting this effort are NEST volunteers, who carry radiation detection equipment stashed inside backpacks and briefcases. Armed with these sensors, as many as 100 two-person teams walk the streets and building hallways searching for the bomb. They wear casual clothes to blend into the crowd, and to avoid frightening the public or alerting the terrorists. As they search, they listen for an alert message that radiation has been detected. The message—"Gamma alert four"—is broadcast from the sensor to a wireless earphone hidden in the volunteer's ear.

Once the bomb is located, and once any terrorists guarding the device are taken care of by the FBI's Hostage Rescue Team or a DoE SWAT team, a special NEST dismantling team

arrives. This group of weapons designers and scientists figure out how to disarm the bomb without making any mistakes or triggering any booby traps. They work closely with units from the Army's 52nd Ordnance Group to create a unique render-safe procedure. After a plan is drawn up, it is then carried out by members of the Army team.

Defusing Danger

The 52nd Ordnance Group is the Army's explosive ordnance disposal arm. Headquartered at Fort Gillem, Georgia, the 52nd responds to major EOD operations around the world, supporting Secret Service efforts, consulting with local law enforcement, and dealing with weapons of mass destruction and sophisticated bombs. The unit, presently under the command of Colonel Mary G. Goodwin, is composed of four battalions which, in turn, are made up of 8 to 10 EOD companies. These companies generally have 23 people organized into six two-man teams, plus a command/support staff, and are located throughout the United States.

As with other military EOD units, the men and women of the 52nd Ordnance Group have successfully attended the joint service EOD school, and completed additional training at Redstone Arsenal. Although every EOD technician in the 52nd is equally capable of handling military ordnance and improvised explosive devices, a handful of soldiers are trained to a much higher level. These individuals walk in the deadly world of improvised nuclear, chemical and biological weapons.

The 52nd currently has four of these teams, known as Weapons of Mass Destruction response units (formerly Special Improvised Explosive Device units). They are located across the country, situated to respond to incidents within 4 hours' notice. These

As you might imagine, dealing with a weapon of mass destruction requires special tools. This is particularly true when you consider that WMD devices are likely to incorporate sophisticated technologies to either trigger detonation or to prevent the bomb from being disarmed. Here's an overview of some of the gear used by EOD techs:

MIRA—A portable device that detects microwave, infrared and acoustic emissions from a distance. Using MIRA, a bomb technician can detect the presence of these types of sensors in a bomb. With this information, he can avoid approaching the device until he figures out how to counter the sensors and devise an appropriate render-safe method.

RONS—Remote Ordnance Neutralization System, a high-tech disrupter that uses a powerful laser beam to neutralize ordnance from a distance. The U.S. Air Force has an operational model stationed in Nevada. RONS is transportable by a Humvee.

PIVS—Portable Integrated Video System, a device that serves as a communications link between an accident/bomb site and the command post. Instantaneous, two-way video and audio information and computer data is transmitted through a fiber-optic cable from the accident site to observers located in a safe area several kilometers away.

Pocket Radiac—A small device that detects and indicates prompt and residual radiation doses received by a bomb tech who is working on a nuclear device or working in a contaminated area. The Navy is currently developing an underwater Radiac for its EOD diver teams.

XM-221—A shaped-charge disrupter made by modifying a submunition from the Army's multiple-launch rocket system.

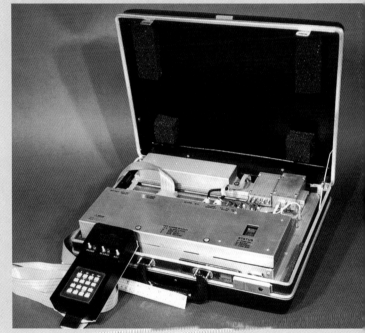

A close-up look at the "guts" of a gamma ray detector posing as a briefcase. *Department of Energy/NOO*

units are the 766th EOD at Cape Canaveral Air Force Station, Florida; 710th EOD in San Diego, California; 797th EOD at Fort Sam Houston, Texas; and the 749th EOD at Andrews Air Force Base, Maryland. All their emergency-response gear is prepackaged and stored on pallets for fast deployment. They work closely with NEST to disarm weapons of mass destruction.

Specifically, WMD technicians help NEST gain access to a device by taking care of any booby traps that might be in the area or physically attached to the bomb itself. They also assist in making a diagnostic evaluation of the weapon, often using robots to take a close look. These remote-controlled vehicles can be outfitted with video cameras, manipulator arms, and nonsparking cutting devices. Portable real-time X-ray sensors are also used to peek under the bomb's casing.

Using this kind of equipment allows scientists and EOD personnel to safely evaluate the bomb from a distance. Since most nuclear bombs require a conventional explosive to start the chain reaction, NEST and WMD units tend to focus on the trigger mechanism. They sweep the outside of the bomb with an EGIS detector, which is a Dustbuster-like device that vacuums up any odors that might be emitted by the bomb. Analysis of these odors by gas chromatography often indicates the type of explosive being used to trigger the bomb.

Once the diagnostic data is reviewed, a plan to disable the bomb is created. This can be achieved in many different ways, including a disrupter shot to the power source or firing mechanism. Regardless of how it is done, the actual procedure is completed by members of the WMD response unit. The bomb is their domain.

In instances when a radiation hazard exists, such as with a radiological bomb, the device is

When a radiation hazard exists, NEST and the 52nd Ordnance Group erect a dense foam barrier over the nuclear bomb. It is designed to contain the radioactive debris and fragments in case the bomb's conventional high explosive detonates. The barrier stands 35 feet tall and has a 50-foot diameter. *Department of Energy/NOO*

enclosed within a 50-foot diameter tent-like cone that stands 35 feet tall. This cone is filled with an aqueous foam, which traps any radioactive debris that is scattered by a conventional explosion.

If the defuzing procedure does not work for some reason, WMD members slip into their bomb suits, wearing a self-contained breathing apparatus. Then they enter the foam to either disarm the bomb by hand or set up the disrupter again for another try.

According to Major James J. Shivers, operations officer for the 52nd, working in the foam is not a pleasant experience, and it is definitely not a place for the claustrophobic. "The foam is not that heavy, but it is confining," he says. "Basically, you have to feel your way in, much like a diver searching the bottom of New York harbor. He can actually see nothing. He's just basically using his hands, feeling. It's not a fun experience."

Deployments

The 52nd Ordnance Group regularly deploys its EOD teams and WMD response units. In 1997, for instance, they responded to 4,200

A member of the 52nd Ordnance Group, 723d Ordnance Company, takes an X-ray of a bomb. The military uses the PS-820 EOD bomb suit to handle IEDs and mines. The suit has a unique visor design: the visor slips into a pocket on the upper chest, rather than being attached to the bomb helmet itself. This supposedly allows the force of an explosion to be absorbed by the bomb tech's upper torso, and not his neck or spine. The visor is also designed so that he can see ordnance and obstacles as close as two feet, without having to bend over. *SF Tomajczyk*

incidents on military posts and 1,802 problems off post. In 1998, there were 3,616 deployments on-post; 2,414 off-post. Most of these events involved military ordnance, improvised explosive devices, or transportation accidents involving explosives or ammunition. Yet, the 52nd has been involved with several domestic terrorism cases also, including:

• The Unabomber—When Theodore Kaczynski was arrested by the FBI on April 3, 1996, at his one-room Montana mountain shack, two teams from the 52nd Ordnance Group helped search the area for bombs and booby traps. The searchers took the precaution of X-raying piles of books and other items to detect any hidden devices. They eventually found two bombs—a "live" package bomb and a partially completed pipe bomb—as well as several firearms, and a plethora of bomb-making items, including chemicals, piping and electrical wire. The incomplete pipe bomb was wrapped in paper and secured with tape.

• The Mountaineer Militia—In October 1996, seven men with ties to the Mountaineer Militia were charged with plotting to bomb the FBI's $200 million national fingerprint records center near Clarksburg, West Virginia, as part of the Militia's "holy war" on the government. EOD teams from the 52nd helped search a militia "safe house" for booby traps and military explosives.

• The Republic of Texas Separatists—After a week-long, armed stand-off with police at Fort Davis, Texas, in the spring of 1997, Texas separatist Richard McLaren, self-proclaimed ambassador of the "Republic of Texas," and three of his followers surrendered to the Texas Rangers after signing a cease-fire agreement. EOD teams from the 52nd Ordnance Group helped search the area. Some 40 to 60 pipe bombs were found in a series of bunkers around the compound. The bomb techs also discovered 10 gasoline cans with explosive coils around them, a propane tank with a pipe bomb attached, 10 rifles and up to 700 rounds of ammunition. The 52nd helped remove these items and rendered safe several booby traps discovered in nearby woods.

Sergeant Peters of the 723d Ordnance Company walks his "dog," an Andros robot. It is capable of picking a bomb up and depositing it inside the unit's total containment vessel. The robot is controlled via tether (as shown here) or by remote control. During the 1996 Olympic Games, the 52nd Ordnance Group provided two EOD technicians for each of the 24 Explosives Diagnostic Teams, as well as robots and bomb trailers. *SF Tomajczyk*

The 52nd Ordnance Group routinely provides its expertise (when approved by the Department of Defense) in support of special events, like the Presidential Inauguration, Republican and Democratic National Conventions, and the G-8 Summit, as well as major sporting events like the Super Bowl.

During the 1996 Olympic Games in Atlanta, for instance, the 52nd provided robots and other EOD gear as well as two EOD technicians for each of the 24 four-man Explosive Diagnostic Teams assigned to various Olympic venues. These plain-clothes teams evaluated and diagnosed suspicious items.

In addition to supporting special events, the 52nd is also involved with dignitary protection. A section of the 52nd, the VIP Protective Support Activity (VIPPSA), coordinates the deployment of military EOD units from all branches of the armed forces to the White House and other locations. Under the direction of the Secret Service, these units help sweep for bombs at sites ahead on the dignitary's schedule.

An EOD contingent is always present at the White House. At any given time, there are at least three two-man teams on station to check the mail and to conduct security sweeps for the President. Each team spends 30 days in the White House's Old Executive Office Building, rotating through four shifts, each about a week long.

VIPPSA also responds to requests from various federal agencies for EOD assistance. So when the Vice President or another high-ranking official is traveling and the Secret Service needs extra EOD teams, it is VIPPSA that takes care of it. They generally assign the task to the military EOD unit(s) nearest the event.

Bugs and Gas

Nuclear terrorism is not the only concern the United States has. There is also the specter of homemade chemical and biological weapons, which are often known as the "poor man's atom bomb," looming over our country. For example, if a biological agent were released in Minnesota's Mall of America, which is visited by people from all over the world, 350,000 people could be infected in a single day.

Officials know that it's only a matter of time before "bugs and gas" are used in this country. Most chem-bio weapons can be made in any basement following simple recipes and using store-bought materials. In the past few years, there have been several "close calls" where extremists threatened to unleash this witches' brew:

• In October 1995, four members of the antigovernment Minnesota Patriots Council were convicted of planning to use ricin, a deadly toxin, to kill government workers. Ricin, which is a derivative of the castor bean, is one of the most poisonous substances known. It can kill through inhalation or ingestion. The extremists had

Army EOD techs have to deal with all sorts of ordnance: from mines to rockets, and from grenades to homemade bombs. Here, a tech carefully clears away the sand from a land mine. *SF Tomajczyk*

enough ricin on hand to kill 1,400 people.

- In November 1995, Larry Harris, an alleged member of the white supremacist group Aryan Nations, plead guilty to possessing three vials of *Yersinia pestis*, the organism that causes bubonic plague. Harris used a fraudulent EPA number and his company's state certification to illegally obtain the bacteria from a biomedical supply lab for $240. Untreated bubonic plague has a case fatality rate of about 60 percent.
- In December 1995, Thomas Lavy, an Army veteran and survivalist, was arrested after 30 federal agents and U.S. Army biological warfare experts raided the Arkansas farm he was staying at. They found 130 grams of ricin on the premises, which was enough to kill 30,000 people.
- In February 1998, an informant alerted the FBI that Larry Harris and William Leavitt, Jr. allegedly had deadly anthrax in their possession. FBI agents arrested them in Henderson, Nevada. Their vehicle was wrapped in plastic and taken to nearby Nellis Air Force Base for testing. Charges against both Harris and Leavitt were dismissed after tests showed the "biological agent" was, in fact, a harmless anthrax veterinary vaccine.
- In July 1998, the FBI arrested three men in Olmito, Texas, for plotting to assassinate President Bill Clinton and other government officials by using a lighter modified to shoot cactus thorns coated with anthrax, botulism, rabies or HIV. The men were charged with federal conspiracy to use a weapon of mass destruction.

Biological agents like tularemia, plague and Q-fever are generally more lethal than chemical weapons because they can affect huge population centers. These agents are also invisible, so you will never know that your city is under attack until days afterward, when people start dropping like flies. It would, in fact, be easy for a lunatic to fly over a city, release a biological agent and then disappear In scenarios like this, it has been determined that 100 pounds of anthrax spores released upwind of a city the size of Des Moines, Iowa, would disable or kill half the population.

What frightens many bomb techs about biological and chemical devices is the fact that they can't see or smell the thing that can kill them. This means they could be walking to their deaths if they approach a device without wearing the proper gear or using special sensors.

The civilian world uses the PAN disrupter to defeat bombs, but the military prefers to use the more powerful 30-millimeter and .50-caliber distrupters. After all, they have to routinely deal with rockets and 500-pound bombs, not 10-pound pipe bombs. *U.S. Army*

The Bug Killers

At this time, the United States relies on the 52nd Ordnance Group and the Army's Technical Escort Unit (TEU) to deal with chemical and biological devices until bomb squads across the country are trained in this hazardous arena. The FBI's Hazardous Devices School intends to train every civilian bomb tech by mid-1999 on how to recognize a chem-bio device by its structure and X-ray image, how to stabilize it, what public safety issues need to be addressed, and what procedures should be taken to contact the military for assistance in dismantling the device.

The Technical Escort Unit is a one-of-a-kind unit that detects, contains, limits the exposure from, and cleans up after a chem-bio attack occurs. It is also equipped to neutralize and dispose of munitions, toxic chemicals and other dangerous materials. The 150-member unit is headquartered at Aberdeen Proving Grounds in Maryland, with attachments at Pine Bluff Arsenal in Arkansas and Dugway Proving Ground in Utah.

It is on call 24 hours a day and maintains two separate response capabilities. The first is the Chemical/Biological Response Team, which consists of 10 specialists who serve as the "first responders" for chem-bio incidents. They can be airborne within 4 hours. The second is the Alert Team, which serves as the advance team for any TEU response. The Alert Team conducts reconnaissance of the site, identifies the chemical or biological agents present, renders any device safe, and assists with small area decontamination. In the event of an emergency, the TEU can muster within 30 minutes and be airborne within 4 hours.

All members of the TEU have been trained to identify chemical agents, how to use decontamination equipment, and how to dispose of chemical agents. They have also received training in radiation safety and how to operate chemical detection equipment, X-ray systems, gas chromatograph/mass spectrometers, and portable isotopic neutron spectroscopic devices.

Additionally, those who specialize in bomb disposal are taught to render safe chem-bio weapons. This is more hazardous than you can imagine, especially when dealing with military-type chemical and biological munitions. According to Army officials, nerve agents (particularly Sarin) become acidic over time and corrode the metal warheads of rockets, mortars, and projectiles in which they are contained. In some cases, the corrosion eats small holes through the metal, allowing the agent or its vapors to escape. If an EOD tech is not taking extreme precautions, he can easily die.

Fortunately, external leaks are detectable by a hand-held sensor known as ICAM (Improved Chemical Agent Monitor), which has a response time of less than 60 seconds. If a technician is dealing with leaking munitions, it is immediately placed in an airtight con-

Members of the 52nd Ordnance Group hone their marksmanship skills with the 5-foot-long, 30-pound M-82A1 Barrett .50-caliber rifle. This powerful weapon is useful in destroying bombs, mines, submunitions and unexploded ordnance at great distances—up to a mile. It sure beats using a PAN disrupter, except for the thrashing it gives your shoulder when you fire it. *52nd Ordnance Group*

When a render-safe shot fails for whatever reason, the 52nd Ordnance Group's WMD Response Teams have to don their bomb suits and put on self-contained breathing apparatus to enter the aqueous foam and rectify the situation. It's definitely not a job for the claustrophobic . . . or the weak-hearted. Since visibility is near zero, you have to rely on touch to figure out what to do. That's not always a wise option where nuclear bombs are concerned. *Department of Energy/NOO*

tainer and then segregated from the other munitions for special storage and disposal. Internal leaks, however, can't be detected without actually taking the device apart. And internal leaks are more dangerous because they can interact with the explosive components, making the warhead more likely to explode during handling or movement.

In January 1993, a construction crew unearthed some World War I-era chemical and high-explosive munitions while digging a sewer line in the exclusive Spring Valley residential area of Washington, D.C. The Army's 52nd Ordnance Group responded and was later joined by the Technical Escort Unit. Together, they removed more than 110 items, including mortars, projectiles and bomb debris. It turned out that the area had been used by the military to train troops in trench warfare and the handling of chemical munitions. After World War I ended, the test pits were buried, along with the munitions, and forgotten.

After evacuating residents from the area, the EOD techs of the TEU and 52nd wore protective clothing to recover the visible munitions, sift through the dirt piles, and segregate the liquid and solid-filled munitions. The 44 suspected chemical rounds were flown by helicopter to Andrews Air Force Base and then air-transported to Pine Bluff Arsenal in Arkansas for storage. The 97 conventional HE rounds were flown to Fort A.P. Hill in rural Virginia and were explosively destroyed.

This incident uncovered a little-known fact: chemical weapons are buried all over America. A 1994 GAO investigation identified 215 burial sites in 33 states that may contain chemical agents, such as Sarin and VX. Most of these states have less than five burial sites, but Utah has 48; Alabama, 35; Maryland, 12; Colorado and Arkansas, 11 each; and Florida and Alaska, 9 each.

Another Spring Valley crisis could occur. And when it does, it will be local bomb squads who will respond to the emergency until the 52nd and the TEU arrive.

Chapter 9

Tools of the Trade

In the early years of bomb disposal, when technicians took the archaic "Rambo" approach of disarming bombs with their bare hands, they were forced to rely more on their wits and bravery than on technology to get the job done. That's all changed with the many scientific advancements that have been applied to bomb disposal equipment. Bomb squads now have a number of high-tech tools available to peer into the innards of a bomb and disarm it from a distance, thereby minimizing the risk to life.

Because of the dangerous environment bomb techs work in, where a single spark can detonate some bombs, EOD equipment must meet unusual standards. For instance, their tools have to be nonsparking and nonmagnetic. Their clothing has to be static-dissipating and flame retardant. Their communication systems cannot emit certain radio frequencies. And, everything must be simple to use while wearing a bulky bomb suit.

Bomb Suits

The bomb suit is the most important piece of equipment that a bomb tech owns. Although it won't save your hide if you're working on a nuclear warhead or a huge 500-pound

> *"You don't want to do this job if you don't have the right tools. It can mean the difference between dying and going home at night."*
>
> —A Bomb Squad Commander

bomb, which is why military EOD techs don't wear bomb suits, it *can* mean the difference between life and death when you're working on a pipe bomb. Bomb suits are made to minimize the danger from explosions.

A variety of companies make bomb suits—Protective Materials Company, Safeco EOD Inc., American Body Armor & Equipment—but the best-known suits are made by Med-Eng Systems Inc. This company conducts intensive, on-going research into blast effects. In fact, Med-Eng Systems' president, Richard L'Abbé, has personally tested his suits by being blown up 19 times with varying amounts of explosives. The result is that Med-Eng suits address four specific threats posed by an exploding bomb: the blast wave, thermal effects, flying fragments, and impact.

The Med-Eng EOD-7B bomb suit, which costs upward of $15,000 and takes 20 weeks to make, consists of a jacket, trousers and a helmet. It features removable laminate ballistic inserts (which protect the neck and the front of the body from fragments) and a back protector that redistributes impact energy away from the spinal column if the bomb tech falls or is thrown into something by an explosion. The entire suit is made so that the materials

A new high-tech explosives-detection portal being developed by Sandia National Laboratories. Known affectionately as the "sniffer," the system takes samples of the air through the holes seen in the photo as a person briefly stands inside the portal. If any traces of explosive compounds are on the person's body or clothing, the sniffer will detect them and sound an alarm. *Sandia National Laboratory*

Resembling more a Knight of the Roundtable than a bomb tech, this photo shows how military EOD technicians used to dress in the past. No bomb tech in his right mind would pick up a suspicious briefcase like this today. Because of the sophistication and lethality of modern bombs, the entire bomb disposal field has adopted a "hands-off, remote disruption" policy. *723d Ordnance Company*

and joints overlap each other. This allows the blast wave to roll over and around the bomb technician rather than through him.

When putting on the EOD-7B suit, the bomb tech starts with the trousers and static-dissipating toe grounder straps, followed by the jacket. Assistants slip in the ballistic inserts, put on the helmet and then plug in the necessary electronics such as environmental controls and communication systems. Affixing the 3/4-inch ballistic visor to the helmet is the last thing the assistants do. Two air hoses

pump fresh air into the helmet. This prevents the visor from fogging and allows the bomb tech to breath easier. A turbo-boost button on the suit's control box, which is carried in a pocket, permits the bomb tech to get a surge of fresh air when needed. This control box also monitors the helmet's communication system, automatically dampening any noise that exceeds 95 decibels.

Depending on the actual configuration, the bomb suit adds 60 to 80 pounds to a bomb technician's weight. Yet, the suit is not cumbersome. Med-Eng demonstrated its suit's flexibility by videotaping a gymnast dressed in an EOD-7B suit performing an acrobatic floor routine, including stints on the parallel bars and pommel horse. One of the reasons the suit is not binding is that its inserts are precurved, allowing full range of motion. Another reason is that the suit places most of its protection on the front side of the bomb tech, not the back. Although this means the bomb tech must back away from a bomb when leaving an area, the lighter weight of the suit is well worth the effort. (Besides, who really wants to turn his back on a bomb?)

Although the suit is not cumbersome, it can be stuffy, especially on hot, humid days. If a bomb tech doesn't take precautions or pay attention to his vital signs, he can succumb to heat exhaustion. For this reason, bomb techs often wear cooling systems under their suits, like ETC's Thermalwear or LSSI's Mark VII Portable Cooling System. Med-Eng offers the BCS-3A and BCS-3R cooling systems, both of which pump cool water through a network of tiny tubes stitched into a stretch-knit shirt, pants and hood assembly. The cooling system, which consists of two or four water bottles, a pump and a power supply, is stored in an insulated bag and hand carried by the bomb tech. If the water is frozen, the BCS-3 systems

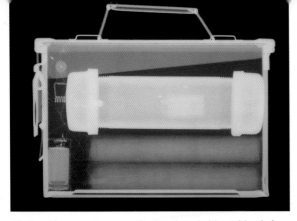

Modern X-ray systems are the bomb techs' best friend. A good picture can tell them exactly how a bomb is made and, more importantly, how they can safely disarm it. This photo shows a pipe bomb with a bare-bulb initiator, along with some dynamite, hidden inside a metal ammunition case. The more sophisticated X-ray systems automatically color-code the wiring, power source, and explosives to make the image easier to "read" by the bomb tech. Some systems even allow a bomb tech to digitally enhance the image. *NAVSCOLEOD*

can keep him cool for up to 100 minutes in 95-degree weather.

In addition to its EOD-7B bomb suit, Med-Eng Systems also makes the SRS-5 suit for reconnaissance purposes. The lightweight outfit, which features an open-design helmet with a thermoformed polycarbonate visor, allows first responders to quickly search a building or an outdoor area for a bomb while wearing some ballistic protection. The FBI likes the suit so much that it has issued it to all of its bomb techs and SWAT teams. If a bomb is found during the initial search, it is then rendered safe by a bomb tech wearing the EOD-7B.

Recognizing the threat posed by chemical and biological agents, Med-Eng has recently produced the EOD-7G biochemical bomb suit. It features a special vapor barrier stitched into the suit's fabric that prevents chemical and biological warfare agents from passing through to the bomb tech. The helmet's visor has also been redesigned to allow a technician to wear a gas mask inside his helmet.

X-Ray Equipment

It's common sense—to disarm a bomb, you have to know how it is made. For bomb techs, the best way to determine this is to X-ray the device and then interpret the film image, tracing out the wires to see what they are connected to.

A popular X-ray machine is the portable XR-150, made by Golden Engineering Inc. Measuring a scant 10 inches long and shaped like an oversized vitamin pill, the XR-150 uses a pulsed 150kV beam that searches a 40-degree, pie-shaped area in front of it. The bomb tech places it in front of the bomb. Then, without touching the device, he carefully positions a Polaroid film plate behind the bomb. When the XR-150 is turned on, it sends radiation through the bomb, and a "picture" of the bomb's innards is captured on film. It takes only a few minutes for the Polaroid to develop.

As any bomb tech can attest, correctly interpreting an X-ray is challenging. Depending on what a bomb is made of, the different densities of the materials used can sometimes create a hazy image on film, potentially blocking important elements from view. To overcome this, bomb techs now use the RTR-3 Portable Digital X-ray Imaging System produced by SAIC. The $21,000 system is composed of three items: a 25-pound briefcase-sized controller unit, a 10-pound X-ray imager (which is a solid-state camera with 8x10-inch viewing area), and an X-ray source.

Once the bomb tech has placed the digital imager and X-ray source on either side of the bomb, he leaves the site. High-resolution black-and-white images of the bomb's components are instantly sent via cable to the briefcase controller and display unit, which can be located several hundred feet away from the bomb. Images can be enhanced by computer

The ATF uses the TR-2000 robot (a.k.a. Max) to handle pipe bombs and other explosive devices. Its small size allows it to be easily transported in the back of an Explosives Enforcement Officer's bomb response vehicle. The robot, like most, can be equipped with a disrupter, to disarm a bomb from a stand-off distance. *Bureau of Alcohol, Tobacco & Firearms*

(e.g., sharpen details, 200–400 percent zoom, grain reduction) so the techs can better evaluate the bomb's construction. It is this ability to assess a bomb from a remote location and enhance an X-ray image that makes the RTR-3 system superior to fluoroscopic and X-ray film devices. Technicians save the digitized image to either a hard drive or a floppy disk. The controller unit can hold 1,700 images in its internal library.

If, for some reason, additional analysis of an image is needed, it can be sent via modem to a bomb squad's headquarters or to the ATF or FBI. This is helpful, for instance, in situations where a bomb tech realizes that he's dealing with a unique fuze. Within minutes, he can send a digitized X-ray image from a bomb site in Des Moines, Iowa, to the FBI in Washington, D.C., and then get suggestions on how to deal with the bomb.

Robots

Mention the word "robot" and people immediately think of *Star War's* R2D2 or the arm-flailing robot in *Lost in Space*. But the robots used by bomb techs are a breed unto themselves, specifically designed to inspect, move and disarm a bomb. The average bomb robot features: a telescoping arm with gripper to pick up a device, move obstacles or open doors; multiple video surveillance cameras (color, infrared, black/white) to send live images back to the bomb techs; mounts for a shotgun or disrupter system; a laser sighting system; an audio system; an X-ray mount assembly; and a tether, fiber optic or wireless control to permit remote operations. Since robots often go into buildings, they are designed to be narrow, lightweight and highly maneuverable. Most robots can do a U-turn in a 39-inch-wide hallway and climb stairs.

A PAN disrupter stands at the ready to blast a metal box and its sticks of dynamite (stashed inside) to kingdom come. Although most disrupters are 12-gauge, an ultraprecise .410-gauge mini-PAN disrupter was specially made for bomb techs who searched the Unabomber's mountain cabin for homemade bombs. *SF Tomajczyk*

The Andros family of robots, made by Remotec, is a popular line of machines. The firm makes several models, which vary in size and capability: the Andros 6x6, Andros 4x4, Andros Mark V-A, Andros Mark VI-A, and the Mini-Andros.

The Mini-Andros is the smallest robot Remotec makes, measuring 16 inches wide and 35 inches long. Its size and weight (60 pounds) make it ideal for transport in the back of a car. In fact, you'll find the Mini-Andros riding around in many FBI bomb-response vehicles. But don't let its small size fool you: The eight-wheeled, tracked robot is highly capable. It can climb over 10-inch-high obstacles, cross 22-inch-wide ditches, navigate 45-degree slopes, move at speeds of 14 inches per second, and lift objects weighing up to 14 pounds. Additionally, the Mini-Andros can be equipped with a 12-gauge shotgun, a PAN disrupter with laser sighting, and an X-ray device. If the robot is used in a nuclear situation, it can also be equipped with a contamination containment box, a smear sampler, and a radiation detector.

The Mini-Andros, like its brothers and sisters, has been used for explosives handling, nuclear surveillance, SWAT operations, airport security, and HazMat response.

Other robot brands include:

- The Rapidex Inc. "Ferret," which was developed under contract with the U.S. Navy for military applications. Its gripper, which has a 10-foot reach, can retrieve objects up to 21 inches wide (like a torpedo) with an adjustable 400-pound clamping force, and its arm can lift in excess of 110 pounds The Ferret features mounts for a semiautomatic shotgun, the Mk-32 X-ray pack, and the double Mk-31 JROD/Mk-2 Dearmer. More than 30 units are in use with the Air Force worldwide. Ferrets are also used by the New York City Police Department and other law enforcement agencies.
- The HDE Robotics Group Inc., TR-2000 enhanced tactical robot, or "Max" for short. Weighing less than 45 pounds, the 10-wheeled robot can be configured to travel in tight places less than 5 inches high (such as under a car). It can also reach heights up to 5 feet. The manipulator arm can lift objects weighing up to 30 pounds close to the chassis and 10 pounds at full extension. As with most robots, the TR-2000 can be outfitted with surveillance cameras, a disrupter, an X-ray device, etc. When operated by radio control, "Max"

The FBI understands that disarming a bomb is a technical activity, often done in a high-risk environment. The Bureau has compiled the following list of safety equipment that every bomb squad in America should have in its arsenal. Note the scope and breadth of items that bomb techs must have available in order to do their job.

Required
    Bomb suit
    Portable X-ray system
    Disrupter/Dearmer
    Demolition Kit
    Hand tools
    Parachute riser cord
    Nylon-filament adhesive tape
    Electrician's tape
    Dental mirror
    Scalpels
    Stethoscope
    Tongue depressor
    Probe (nonconductive)
    Hemostats
    Candle and matches

Recommended
    Bomb disposal robot
    Bomb truck
    Bomb trailer
    Camera and tape recorder
    Portable lighting system
    Hydraulic jack
    Portable generator
    Shovels, rakes and sifting equipment
    Self-contained breathing apparatus
    Cooling vest for bomb suit
    Electric drill
    Communication equipment
    Rigging and rope equipment
    Pulleys and clamps
    Evidence collection kit
    Metal detector
    Gloves (fire and chemical resistant)
    Tyvek protective clothing
    Reference publications

Source: FBI Bomb Data Center

has a range of up to 1,000 yards. The TR-2000 is used by the ATF, FBI, NASA, the Air Force and a variety of emergency response teams.

- The Terra Aerospace Corporation "Cerberus" EOD robot features three independent telescoping booms, one for a pan/tilt camera, another for the manipulator arm, and the last for a weapon or disrupter. The six-wheeled robot can pull or drag objects weighing up to 400 pounds and lift objects weighing as much as 110 pounds The Cerberus has a vertical reach of 7 feet and a top speed of 5 miles per hour.

Disrupters

In the world of bomb disposal, the disrupter is the primary tool of a bomb tech. Resembling a small jungle gym, a disrupter is essentially a gun barrel affixed to a tripod. It is designed to fire various types of projectiles at a bomb, with the intention of preventing it from exploding. A bomb tech does this by aiming the barrel at a particular component of the bomb, such as the power source or the fuze, in order to "disrupt" that component and prevent the bomb from detonating.

There are several types of disrupters on the market today. The most widely used is the Percussion-Actuated, Nonelectric (PAN) disrupter, which is distributed by Ideal Products Inc. Unlike other disrupters, the PAN disrupter fires its projectiles at adjustable speeds to match the bomb's strength of construction, *without* causing detonation. For example, a steel plug may be fired toward a pipe bomb at 1,500 feet per second with the goal of ripping an end cap off, but the same steel plug might be fired at a briefcase bomb at only 500 feet per second with the intent of destroying the battery. Having control over the projectile's speed helps prevent accidental detonation of the bomb, which is a problem sometimes experienced with other disrupter models.

The FBI is so impressed with the PAN disrupter's capabilities that it has purchased and distributed the device to bomb squads across the nation.

The PAN disrupter is very flexible: It can be adjusted to compensate for both height and angle. It can be fired with an electrical, safety fuse or squib firing mechanism. A laser sight, affixed to the barrel, allows the bomb tech to aim at a specific component inside the bomb. The PAN is not a one-time-use tool. Like a gun, the stainless steel device can be fired multiple times without having to be replaced.

As for ammunition, the PAN disrupter shoots a wide variety of high-, low- and medium-velocity projectiles, including lead and steel shot, hollow point slugs, bean bags, solid steel slugs, and disintegrating projectiles. All are based on a standard 12-gauge shotgun shell.

Blank cartridges are used to shoot water and other liquids. Compressed water can do tremendous damage, especially to packages and lightweight metal. In fact, water charges are used more often by bomb techs than any other type of projectile. One of the more interesting liquid rounds is the "Snot" round. A polymer is added to thicken the water, allowing it to hold together longer and at greater distances compared to normal water.

Another type of liquid disrupter is the Mineral Water Bottle disrupter system, more commonly referred to as the "Black Box." It consists of two or three bottles (500 milliliter or 1.5 liters in size) filled with water. An explosive charge, such as Detcord or C-4 plastic explosive, is carefully placed around the bottles to ensure even detonation. When the charge explodes, the compressed water travels outward in a 360-degree blast. Unlike the

Four sticks of dynamite explode inside a single-vent containment vessel. As can be clearly seen, the blast is directed vertically from the pot. With a high-pitch whistle, the blast wave screeches nearly a mile into the atmosphere, a white smoke ring following. This photo was taken at the FBI's Hazardous Devices School in Alabama. *SF Tomajczyk*

surgical PAN disrupter, which places its charge in a very precise manner, the Black Box takes a less sophisticated "bulldozer" approach. It is used to blast apart packages in the hope of exposing the bomb and disrupting its sensitive components.

In the PAN disrupter system, projectiles are matched with different bomb types: steel slugs are used against pipe bombs, bean bags against PVC-encased devices, and water against briefcases, packages and lightweight metal. The speed of the projectile is adjusted, depending on whether a bomb tech wants to

An FBI total containment vessel on wheels. Attached to a motorized frame, the TCV can literally be driven down the trailer ramp (left) and into a building where it rides the elevators to the location of a discovered bomb. The bomb tech steers the vehicle from a rear platform area. *Federal Bureau of Investigation*

destroy an object or limit the amount of damage so as to preserve forensic evidence.

Of course, there are other disrupters on the market besides the PAN. Royal Arms makes the RADC Cannon (which is quite similar to the PAN), Sig/Zilla Inc. makes a .750 disrupter, and Ithaca Acquisition Corp. makes the Mark I and Mark II disrupters. These disrupters vary in capability, and range in weight from 25 to 60 pounds. Prices range from $1,300 to $3,000 for these disrupters and for PAN disrupter kits. The price generally includes the barrel, a stand, the firing mechanism and some ammunition.

Bomb Disposal Transport Trailers

Once a bomb is found, the bomb tech has several options—blow it in place with counptercharges; defuze it and make it safe where it lies; move it to another location to be destroyed or disarmed. The final decision depends on the situation. For instance, if a pipe bomb is found in a vacant field, it will probably be blown in place. But if the pipe bomb is in a crowded building, it will be removed so that bystanders are not injured and the building is not damaged. In this situation, the bomb is transported by a trailer.

There are three types of bomb containment vessels: single vent, double vent and total containment. In a single vent, which resembles an oversized can with its top removed, the blast wave is directed upward when the bomb detonates. The double-vent acts in a similar fashion, but the blast wave is directed both upward and downward. Both of

A portable incinerator that consumes ammunition and Class C fireworks. Made by Hurd's Custom Machinery, the device can burn 100-pounds of ammo ranging from .22- to .50-caliber shells in a matter of minutes using LP gas. Bomb techs often come across ammo when clearing a terrorist's safe house. *Hurd's Custom Machinery*

these containers are composed of two independent steel tubes with space between, which is generally filled with sand or vermiculite to help "deaden" the blast's outward effects. The inside bomb tube is about 34 inches in diameter; the bomb is suspended on netting in the center of the tube.

Hurd's Custom Machinery, Inc., perhaps the best-known builder of bomb trailers, has been in business since 1947. The company produces three models, the 100, 200, and 300. Depending on the model, they range from 15 to 20 feet in length and feature such amenities as a robot transport area, built-in toolbox and hoist, remote control loading capability, a lighting system, an electric power capstan winch, and a robot loading ramp. Hurd's also manufactures a portable incinerator that is capable of destroying ammunition and fireworks. The incinerator can consume 100 pounds of ammo in just a few minutes.

In situations where single- and double-vented containers are impractical to use, such as at major public events or crowded city environments where a blast wave may still cause considerable damage, bomb techs use the Total Containment Vessel (TCV). Produced by Nabco, Inc., the TCV is designed to fully suppress an explosion. There is no blast wave and there are no fragments. About the only thing the person on the street sees during an explosion is hot, white gas hissing through some vents.

The TCV itself is a large sphere made from high-strength, high-impact steel that has a thickness of 1.5 inches. The inner diameter of

Resembling a Dustbuster vacuum, the EGIS detector is swept over a suspect item by a bomb tech or forensic chemist. The device sucks fumes into a small canister that is removed and placed inside a gas chromatograph, which identifies the chemical composition of the odors. In a matter of minutes, investigators are able to determine whether or not an explosive is present and, if so, which one. The ATF routinely uses this detector to determine if a package contains an explosive, as well as to identify the type of explosive used at a bomb scene. *SF Tomajczyk*

Is this man crazy? Nope. He's Richard L'Abbé, president of Med-Eng Systems. He has been blown up 19 times testing his company's bomb suit to make sure it offers bomb techs the best protection possible. *SF Tomajczyk*

"Blowing yourself up is the ultimate high," said Richard L'Abbé, president of Med-Eng Systems in Ottawa, Canada. And he should know; he's been blown up 19 times since 1985 while testing his company's bomb suits. You see, he wants to make certain that their state-of-the-art suit offers bomb technicians the highest protection possible.

The first bomb L'Abbé confronted as a human guinea pig was in the spring of 1985. Med-Eng Systems was conducting a week-long series of tests to learn more about blast effects on the human body so that future bomb suit enhancements could be made. The tests involved placing a sensor-loaded mannequin near an explosive charge and then detonating

it. The scientists collected data on overpressure, heat and fragmentation from the safety of a nearby bunker. By the third day of testing, Richard's curiosity got the best of him.

"I decided that I'd try putting on the suit myself and getting close to an explosive just to see what it felt like."

He wasn't crazy, he had a valid reason for doing it. When he gave presentations to bomb techs about the capabilities of his company's equipment, he nearly always had someone second-guessing him. Many of them didn't believe in bomb suits to begin with, convinced that they were really body bags.

So Richard strapped on a bomb suit and stood in for the test dummy.

A mechanical engineer by training, Richard didn't feel he was in danger of being injured, because he had carefully analyzed the graphs and calculated the blast pressures. Nonetheless, he was nervous when he found himself face-to-face with 2 pounds of dynamite.

"I had a good idea of what kind of pressures would cause what level of injuries," he explained, "But when you go from a theoretical graph approach to standing in front of this charge yourself, it's a very different matter. I hoped that I did my math right."

As the countdown neared zero, Richard braced himself. BLAM!

The dynamite exploded and, almost simultaneously, the blast wave pummeled his body. Then, just as quickly, it was over. The test had lasted only milliseconds. Richard hadn't lost consciousness and he hadn't been bowled over. He straightened himself up and quickly patted himself down to make sure that he wasn't injured. He was relieved to find that he was okay.

"My first thought was, 'Whew! That wasn't so bad.'"

And so, the next day, he did it again . . . this time much closer, only 15 feet away from the dynamite. What did it feel like to be blown up?

"It's hard to describe," he said, struggling to find the right words. "It's like a small truck hitting you, but it lasts only a fraction of a second. It sends quite a vibration into you."

Since that day, he has done tests around the world to prove that Med-Eng bomb suits work. The largest explosion that he's endured was 4.5 pounds of dynamite.

"That was actually quite painful," he said. "Something I'll never do again. I got a pretty bad headache out of that one."

Actually, the headache proved to be a good thing. Richard asked his R&D team to investigate why he sometimes got a headache after being blown up. Using mannequins fitted with accelerometers, they soon had the answer: an ailment they called Blast Induced Head Acceleration. When a bomb explodes, the head is thrown violently backward. Since the brain, skull and tissues are made of different materials with varying densities, they accelerate at different speeds. The result is that the brain is sloshed around inside the skull, resulting in bruising and, subsequently, severe headaches.

This discovery led Med-Eng Systems to redesign its bomb helmet to better absorb the shock. The firm continues to do aggressive research into the dynamics of explosions, so that its line of bomb suits offer greater protection from heat, fragments, impact and pressure.

"It's only by investing in R&D that you can expect your products to improve," he said. "The more you test, the more you learn. And the more you learn, the more you can improve your equipment. The safety of the bomb technician is paramount. No product goes out the door until it is fully tested and perfected."

All the research that Med-Eng Systems and Richard L'Abbé have done has resulted in gains for the bomb disposal industry. For instance, knowledge about how an explosion affects the bomb suit and the human body have encouraged bomb squads to remotely defuse bombs with robots and disrupters.

"It was a real turning point," said L'Abbé, "Because they (now) realize that the methods that they had historically been using were quite dangerous. Some of them used to dismantle bombs by hand. Now they know that distance is their best friend."

"I'd like to think that we have contributed to bomb technicians coming home at night to their families."

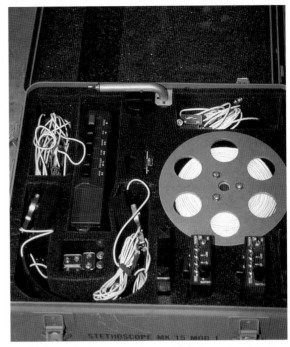

An ultra-sensitive electronic stethoscope helps bomb techs listen in to what is going on inside a bomb or suspicious package. It's much better (and safer!) than pressing an ear to the device. *SF Tomajczyk*

the sphere is either 42 inches or 64 inches, depending on the model. Bombs are positioned inside the sphere by robot through a 21.5-inch round door. The bomb lays in a disposable basket. Once it is placed inside the sphere and the door is remotely closed by a winch, the TCV can be moved to a safe detonation site.

The TCV was developed for the U.S. government and first appeared at the 1984 Summer Olympic Games in Los Angeles. Since then, it has been used by the FBI, Secret Service, U.S. Army, U.S. Navy, U.S. Air Force and a host of bomb squads, including Metro Dade, Dallas, Raleigh, Los Angeles, and Baltimore. It is also used by the National Institutes of

Health, Michigan State Police, Chicago O'Hare International Airport, Dallas-Fort Worth International Airport, and Orange County Sheriff's Department.

All TCVs are tested with 10 pounds of explosive before being sold to ensure that there are no faults in the construction. Like the single- and double-vented bomb trailers, a TCV must be replaced when its sphere distorts or cracks from an explosion. Obviously, this occurs much sooner than it does for the single- and double-vented trailers. Depending on the size of the bombs, the life expectancy of a TCV is only about seven explosions. It must be discarded when there is more than a 3 percent stretch on the outer shell.

As a result of the threat posed by chemical and biological agents, Nabco has modified its TCV so that it can operate as a gas-tight system. This means there is absolutely no venting after detonation. Bomb techs place the bomb inside the TCV, shut the sphere's two doors, and then disrupt the bomb. Samples of the interior atmosphere are taken to determine if a chemical or biological agent is present. If so, the sphere is filled with a decontaminant and flushed out. This chem-bio TCV was on hand during the 1996 Olympic Games in Atlanta.

And All the Rest

There is a plethora of items on today's market that bomb techs can rely on to do their jobs quickly, efficiently and safely. Some of the more mundane but important items include electronic stethoscopes to listen to the innards of a bomb, protective shields to hide behind when approaching a device, rigging to remotely move a bomb through a building and place it inside a bomb trailer, explosives to countercharge a bomb, and telescoping, hand-held manipulators that enable a bomb tech to grab a small bomb from 10 to 15 feet away.

Bomb techs are masters of rigging. Using rope and break-away pulleys, a good bomb tech can safely navigate a bomb through a building's twisting hallways and into a bomb trailer from hundreds of feet away. You'll find rigging equipment and basic hand tools in every bomb truck. *SF Tomajczyk*

When things become more dangerous, such as clearing unexploded military ordnance or hazardous materials, bomb techs often resort to remote control kits. OAO Robotics makes a kit that allows a regular bulldozer, skid loader, forklift, or excavator to be adapted for remote operation. The system is controlled by a custom microprocessor card, which simultaneously operates numerous functions. This means that a bulldozer can be "told" to lower its blade and move forward while turning to the left . . . all at the same time. The remote control kit eliminates human exposure to a deadly environment, while increasing efficiency and minimizing costs.

ANFO—Ammonium Nitrate/Fuel Oil, an explosive mixture.

BIP—Blow In Place. To detonate an explosive or bomb where it's found using a countercharge to do so.

Black Box—A broad-area disrupter made from water bottles and an explosive charge. It is used to open briefcases and packages.

Blow And Go—Military phrase meaning for an EOD team to quickly countercharge a piece of ordnance where it lies and then continue on with the mission, rather than attempt to disarm it. See also BIP.

CBIRF—Chemical/Biological Incident Response Force, a 350-member Marine Corps unit that was created in 1996 to respond to chemical and biological attacks.

Cookie Cutter, Magic Cube—Nicknames for special, high-tech devices created at Sandia National Laboratory to enable bomb techs to defeat improvised explosive devices. See also Black Box and Disrupter.

Blaster—Slang for a bomber who knows what he's doing.

Clayvon—Trademark for a type of specialty disintegrating round used in 12-gauge disrupters. The slug is composed of clay and powdered steel.

Cook-Off Point—A preplanned location in a city where a bomb can be taken and safely detonated.

Crab—Nickname for the Explosive Ordnance Disposal badge because, at a distance, it resembles the saltwater crustacean. The badge is awarded to military personnel who complete the joint service EOD course.

Dead Bug Drill—An exercise that teaches bomb techs how to get back up on their feet while wearing a 60- to 80-pound bomb suit.

Disrupter—A tripod-mounted, gun-like device that shoots water, solid slugs or specialty rounds (e.g., bean bag, frangible slug) at a bomb, thereby preventing it from detonating as designed. See also PAN Disrupter, and Black Box.

DoE—Department of Energy

Downwind Team—Nickname for any one of several units that respond to a nuclear, chemical or biological incident.

EOD—Explosive Ordnance Disposal, the military's equivalent of a civilian "bomb squad."

ERT—Evidence Response Team, an FBI asset that responds to bombing incidents and other crime scenes to collect criminal evidence. Bomb technicians are often included on ERTs because of their knowledge about bomb construction and components.

Felix—Nickname for a bomb tech, after the cat with nine lives.

Floater—Navy slang for a floating mine.

Fuse—A burning time fuse.

Fuze—A device that initiates the detonation of an explosive device. A fuze can be mechanical, electrical or electronic in nature. A clock is an example of a mechanical fuze.

Get Bit—To become a casualty of a chemical or biological agent.

HEU—Highly Enriched Uranium

IED—Improvised Explosive Device, a bomb made from commonly available items (e.g., pipe bomb).

IND—Improvised Nuclear Device, a homemade nuclear bomb.

Load And Go—To remove injured bombing victims from the scene as quickly as possible, while providing the absolute minimum medical treatment necessary. The scene is evacuated until a search for secondary devices is conducted.

Magic Cube—see Cookie Cutter

Master Blaster—Nickname for a Master EOD technician in the military.

Merk—Short for "mercury switch." Liquid mercury is used in some bombs to complete the electric circuitry when the device is moved, hence triggering detonation. This is a sophisticated detonation technique.

Molly—Slang for Molotov cocktail.

NEST—Nuclear Emergency Search Team, a Department of Energy unit that locates and disarms nuclear devices.

Open Pot—Nickname for a single- or double-vented bomb container.

Ordnance—Military explosive weapons of war, including bombs, mines, rockets, grenades, and ammunition.

PAN Disrupter—Percussion-Actuated, Nonelectric disrupter. A precision-shot disrupter that allows the bomb tech to match the ammo by type and velocity with the bomb so as to prevent detonation. See also Disrupter.

Pig Tail—The knot used to tie a length of det-cord to a main trunk.

Pink Cloud—What you become if you're too close to a bomb when it explodes.

Radiological Bomb—Dynamite or plastic explosive that is laced with radioactive material.

Render Safe—To make an explosive device unable to detonate as intended by its builder. Different bombs have different RSPs for bomb technicians to follow.

RSP—Render-safe procedure.

Scent Cone—The downwind waftings of an explosive that dogs learn to detect. The size and shape of the scent cone depends on the wind strength. By zig-zagging upwind through the scent cone, a dog can find the bomb.

Seat—The location of a bomb when it detonates (a.k.a. seat of the explosion).

Semtex—A Czechoslovakian plastic explosive popular with terrorists.

Signature—Identifying features in how a bomb is constructed that reveals to investigators who the maker is. Bombers often use the same containers, wiring techniques, and components when building a device.

Site 39—A CIA facility located at Hertford, North Carolina, where a variety of advanced courses are taught to federal and military operatives. Both the ATF and FBI teach bomb-related courses here.

Slimed—To be exposed to a chemical warfare agent.

Snot—A polymer liquid that is used as a disrupter charge. Snot holds together better and longer than ordinary water, allowing for stand-off shots. See also Disrupter and Water Charge.

Soak Time (Wait Time)—The amount of time following an explosion to ensure that a second device is not around, or the time a bomb is monitored to ensure that a render-safe procedure has worked. The length of soak time varies, depending on the situation.

TCV—Total Containment Vessel, a spherical bomb container that suppresses the blast and traps debris and shrapnel. It is often used in city environments.

Time on Target—The actual time spent up-close and personal with an explosive device. Bomb techs limit their time on target as much as possible.

TSWG—Technical Support Working Group, a federal interagency program established to identify and develop technologies to thwart acts of terrorism. This includes the prototype development of EOD tools to render safe weapons of mass destruction.

Uncle Fester—A person who publishes or shares information on how to make an improvised chemical device. These people often use the Internet to do this.

UXO—Unexploded Ordnance.

Water Charge—A type of shot used to render safe a bomb. A small amount of water—150 milliliters or so—is fired at the bomb at speeds of more than 500 feet per second. Since water cannot be compressed, it acts as a solid, ripping the bomb's container apart. Shaped water charges have been known to penetrate half-inch steel plates. See also Disrupter and Snot.

Witches' Brew—Slang for a chemical agent or an explosive mixture, such as ANFO.

WMD—Weapons of Mass Destruction, which are devices that use nuclear warheads or deadly chemical or biological agents to kill a large number of people.